KATHLEEN WHYTE
embroiderer

LIZ ARTHUR

KATHLEEN WHYTE
embroiderer

B T Batsford Limited London

ISBN 0 7134 5578 0

Typeset by Servis Filmsetting Limited, Manchester
and printed in Great Britain by
Anchor Brendon Ltd
Tiptree, Essex
for the publishers
B T Batsford Limited
4 Fitzhardinge Street
London W1H 0AH

Contents

Preface

My interest in embroidery developed from the study of the history of dress, and through involvement in the organization of several exhibitions and a closer practical study of modern embroidery I began to appreciate the subtleties and difficulties of this form of expression, as well as the achievement of professional embroiderers, foremost among them Kathleen Whyte. Since part of the fascination of any art form is the ideas and thought processes of the artist, I offer no apologies for quoting extensively from her own words which she uses so concisely and aptly in her own inimitable way. This book is therefore written as an appreciation of Kathleen Whyte's contribution to the moving pattern of embroidery.

Glasgow 1988   E A

Acknowledgment

I would like to thank the following former students and staff of Glasgow School of Art for their kind and generous help: Miss Crissie White, Mrs Hannah Frew Paterson, Mrs Carol Jones, Mrs Midge Gourlay, Mrs Kirsty McFarlane, Mrs Betty Myerscough, Mrs H Crawford (Kathleen Mann), Mrs Marion Stewart, Mr Malcolm Lochhead and Mr Robert Stewart.

For allowing me to photograph their embroideries I thank Mr and Mrs John Wallace, Mr and Mrs W Chalmers Brown, Mrs Betty Semple, Mrs Molly Kerr, Miss Margaret Brodie, Miss Betty Whyte, Mr Malcolm Lochhead, the Rev Iain Telfer, the Rev George Fairlie, Miss Naomi Tarrant, Assistant Keeper of Costume and Textiles at the Royal Museums of Scotland and her assistant Miss Amanda Scott. I am especially grateful to Miss Ellen Howden and Mr Jim Stewart for their photography. Thanks are also due to the *Dundee Courier*, *Crafts Magazine* and Glasgow Museums and Art Galleries for allowing me to reproduce their photographs.

I am indebted to the Embroiderers' Guild for allowing me to quote at length from *Embroidery Magazine*, to Miss Betty Whyte for her help and advice and Mrs Suzanne Finn for typing this book.

In particular I would like to thank Kathleen Whyte for her generosity in allowing me to use her photographs and to photograph her work, but most of all for her kindness in answering my endless questions with patience and courtesy. Finally, I thank my husband, Bill, for his support and patience.

Glasgow 1988   E A

The publisher acknowledges subsidy from the Scottish Arts Council towards the publication of this volume.

Note to illustrations
Height precedes width.
Measurements are given in inches with centimetres in brackets.
Descriptions are followed by the name of the owner.
All work illustrated is by Kathleen Whyte unless otherwise stated.

Introduction

Since its inception in 1894 the embroidery department of Glasgow School of Art with its succession of remarkable teachers has played a major role in the development of embroidery. At a time when there was criticism that British Art Schools were not producing students whose designs were fitted to the material and purpose they served, its founder Jessie Newbery broke with Victorian tradition and established the department which laid the foundation of a radical new attitude to embroidery design. She condemned designers who believed that beauty lay in the elaboration of design and laborious execution. Her students produced simplified, stylized designs based on plant forms which were translated into stitchery and appliqué, often combined with lettering or needleweaving. These carefully prepared designs were invariably used to embellish articles of dress such as large collars, or household items such as cushions and portieres which were an important feature of the interiors of the day. Many architects, including Charles Rennie Mackintosh and M H Baillie Scott, produced embroidery designs and used embroidery as an integral part of their interior schemes.

Under the sympathetic directorship of Francis Newbery embroidery flourished and became the most important craft subject taught in the School. The work developed distinctive characteristics and there was a similarity in the work produced by the students, although there were individual differences in the quality of design and standard of craftsmanship. From the beginning the classes were not confined to students, but open to anyone with an interest in embroidery. With the introduction of Saturday classes for primary and secondary school teachers, needlework became a general requirement for all women teachers in the West of Scotland. The department won critical acclaim in publications such as *The Studio* and its influence became very widespread, particularly after Ann Macbeth succeeded Jessie Newbery in 1908. She made a great contribution as a teacher, through her books and as a lecturer. Her influence on her students was profound and her most notable contribution to the syllabus was the introduction of figures which she regarded as the supreme challenge for the embroiderer. The very fine draughtsmanship of her own figure panels is obvious but it is possible to see that later, in the less competent hands of the amateur, these romantic figures degenerated into the 'crinoline ladies' too often seen on tray cloths and chair backs.

From 1920 Anne Knox Arthur continued the work of Jessie Newbery and Ann Macbeth but the embroidery produced had lost its originality and although still of a very high standard was almost indistinguishable from that produced in

Kathleen Whyte in her studio at her loom, 1985
Courtesy Crafts Magazine

Liverpool or Birmingham. With her retirement in 1930, Kathleen Mann, who trained at Croydon School of Art with Rebecca Crompton, became head of the department. Although she only remained for four years she revitalized the department by the introduction of fresh, lively ideas. She too produced several books as well as interesting work which was featured in *The Studio*. In the late 1930s the department took on another aspect with the introduction of weaving by Agnes McCredie. Her successor Kathleen Whyte shared many of the views of Jessie Newbery and Ann Macbeth, such as the importance of design and the maintenance of the highest standards of craftsmanship and that embroidery should not be a slave to tradition but should express the spirit of its own age.

In keeping with this view she has fostered an individuality of expression in the work of each of her students which is an important aspect of her unique contribution to the department of Glasgow School of Art.

1 The formative years 1909-32

Helen Kathleen Ramsay Whyte was born in Arbroath on the east coast of Scotland in August 1909. Her father was the youngest of nine children of a master joiner. He and his brothers became engineers. Succeeding generations have all tended to be 'good with their hands', inventive and ingenious with a high proportion of craftspeople, architects and engineers among them. From her mother came not only good quality Edwardian standards and the technique of sewing and putting things together, but also something much rarer – aesthetic excitement. From humble beginnings she had acquired the skills needed to be a lady's maid and found employment with county families whom she accompanied to Italy on their seasonal visits in the heyday of such activities. With an absorbent and retentive mind she drank up the magic of Rome and Venice and developed an unfeigned appreciation of cultured things. Therefore the house Kathleen grew up in was full of good books, pictures, fabrics and talk of Italy.

Her mother enjoyed 'real things' such as the finest Shetland shawls, handmade lace and embroidery and fine damask linen ordered directly from Ireland. She was always making things and her daughter's earliest efforts at embroidery at the age of four were 'outlining animals stamped on coloured linen in stem stitch which behaved well on simple shapes like a pig, but gave a lot of trouble on feathery chickens'.[1] Later when Kathleen went to school in Arbroath she followed the set curriculum based on the system devised by Ann Macbeth and Margaret Swanson which was published in their book *Educational Needlecraft* in 1911. This course gave little scope for individuality and she made a bag like those made by every other girl. 'A pattern of squares and diamonds evolved to make a border by sewing with large stitches from one pencil dot to the next on unbleached calico. This bag, especially when it acquired white silk ribbons, did not fit in with her ambitions which although hazy were real.'[2] Despite this she later enjoyed some techniques such as making good buttonholes and was intrigued by stroking gathers into a band. This delight in craftsmanship and her abilities to draw and make things were to increase with time.

From 1911-13 and 1920-23 the rest of the family joined her father who was working in India (*1*). The move to Jamshedpur made a considerable impact on the young Kathleen who already had a strong visual awareness. The rich variety of textiles and brilliant colours made particularly vivid impressions on her. 'There were no shops or easily reached bazaars so our excitements were occasioned by visits of Box Wallahs who would bring their merchandise in huge bundles to spread on the verandah and display it with tempting skill. . . . Many qualities of tussore silk in natural shades, vividly coloured pieces and some strange stuff, one I remember was pineapple silk, a type of gauze, these and many more were spread around. Life moved slowly and there was plenty of time to look and enjoy. Other more modest types of merchants

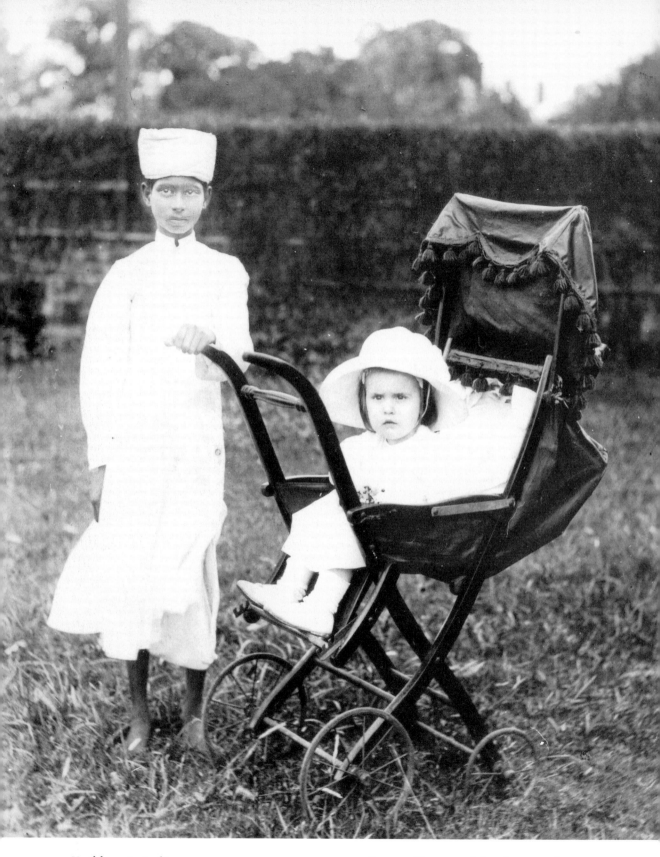

1   *Kathleen in India, 1912*   2   *Loreto Convent School, Darjeeling*

would bring a wide selection of white cottons, neatly done up in bolts of probably a dozen yards, banded with gaily coloured labels and rejoicing in special names such as nainsook and madapolam.'[3]

This stay in India and the resulting quantities of local white embroidery, Chikan work, in their home reinforced her natural intuitive appreciation of textiles and fostered an ability to recognise different types of embroidery.

On the second visit to India she went as a boarder to the Loreto Convent School in Darjeeling where the girls stayed for nine months at a time, being so far from home (2). The school, situated in the foothills of the Himalayas, was finally reached by a tiny narrow gauge railway with open sided carriages after the journey from Calcutta which involved several changes of train. A short train journey from the school was Ghoom, and once a year the girls would walk to Tiger Hill and have a picnic in view of Mount Everest. This was a large event with coolies carrying baskets of food. The stay at Loreto was enjoyable because although strict the nuns gave the girls a great deal of freedom. A school essay written later in Arbroath gives a vivid picture of the long journey from Darjeeling to Calcutta. The following extract describes the lively and no doubt noisy group of girls:

'We had quite a long walk to the station and when we reached it the train was waiting and we immediately began to tumble ourselves and our belongings into the compartments. We then commenced to take in a store of oranges and monkey nuts which we bought from the little Butia women who came selling them. The nuts cost one pice (farthing) a packet and we bought such an amount that we could easily have been mistaken for young monkeys or squirrels laying in their winter hoard, and we bought canes to switch all the plants within reach from the train.'

Sewing was very much encouraged at Loreto Convent and Kathleen was given a good grounding in techniques. In her free time she learned to do Hardanger work and also made a dress in darned net for her younger sister, devising the patterns herself with the help of a Needlework Encyclopaedia (3).

There were also special drawing classes in which the girls 'used paper stumps to apply powdered charcoal from small chamois leather palettes' and 'craft' classes in which Kathleen painted cherries on black taffeta to make a tea cosy. Her overwhelming memory of this environment is of the 'extraordinary natural beauty of the whole place, the great feeling of space in the surrounding landscape and the grandeur of the snow clad range of mountains, forever with us.'[4] She was also intrigued by the clothes of the Bhutia people: 'with their rosy cheeks and heavy skirts, felt boots and the rather jaunty hats, quilted and fur trimmed, worn by the men. The women carrying immense bundles from headbands on their foreheads had their hands free to knit garishly coloured stockings in what seemed to be elaborate, raised patterns'.[5]

From 1923–27 on the family's return from India Kathleen attended Arbroath High School where the teaching in the Art Department 'was robust and purposeful with a design content not untinged by Art Nouveau'.[6] In her final year she embroidered a large figure panel of Saint Elizabeth of Bohemia, a subject idea suggested by conversations with her mother. Many years later she discovered that this had been a favourite subject of her distinguished predecessor Ann Macbeth.

On leaving school Kathleen went to Gray's School of Art, Aberdeen where she took the Diploma Course in General Design. This four year course was introduced into the four Scottish Art Schools in 1920. It was different from corresponding English courses in that the staff had much more freedom, being allowed to organise their own courses with guidance from external assessors who submitted reports to the schools and the Scottish Education Department. This design course had a wider outlook than previously, it was broadly based for the first two years and included life drawing, design, lettering, sculpture and murals and, in the evenings, jewellery and other craft classes. Gradually there was greater specialization, with the chosen sub-

3 *Dress of cotton net made for her sister in*
1922–23. It would have been worn over a silk
or cotton petticoat with a ribbon sash.
Length 20 (51)
Glasgow Museums and Art Galleries

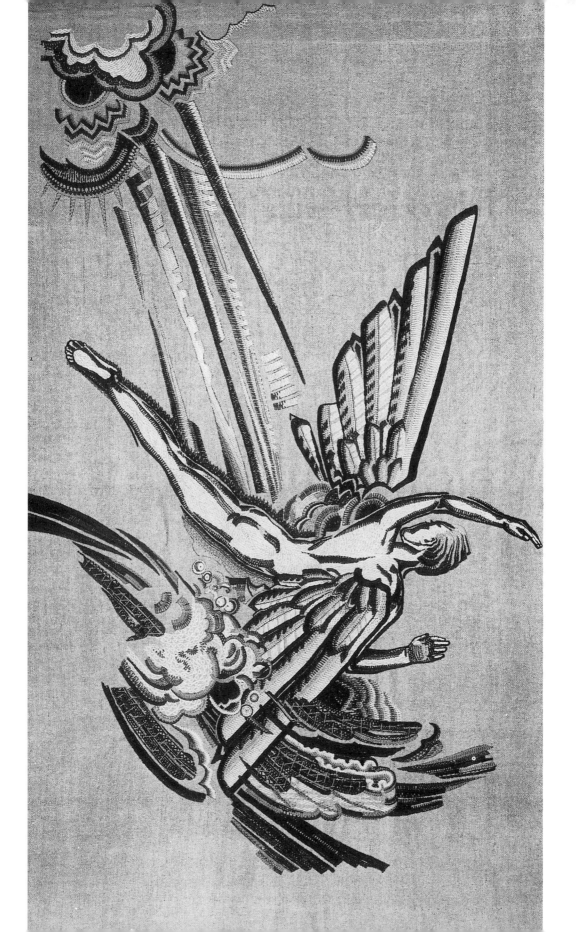

4 Icarus *1932*
Worked in a wide variety of stitches including
Roumanian and herringbone which are used
for the wing feathers. Darning suggests the
body contours and the brightly coloured
wools are in organized gradations of tone.
100 × 50 (254 × 127)
Royal Museums of Scotland

5 Icarus *1932*
Detail of the inventive and assured use of
stitchery to represent the turbulent movement
of the sea. See colour plate 2

ject assuming more importance. Along with all Art School subjects embroidery was enjoying a revival in the late 1920s after a period in the doldrums.

In Britain in the years immediately after the First World War there had not been the vigorous fine art development that had occurred on the continent, which had regarded the war as cathartic and had given the intellectual basis and impetus to a new style of architecture and design. Although The Bauhaus eventually had a profound impact on British design theory and practice, initially its new ideas were viewed with suspicion because they were foreign. There had been no political disruption in Britain as there had been in Europe and there was a desire to preserve the status quo or return to the idyllic days of the Edwardian era. But these new European ideas symbolised change and had socialist overtones, therefore they were seen as a threat or, at the very least, an irrelevance. The result, in Britain, was a nostalgic continuation of the arts and crafts tradition established by William Morris and a preponderance of eclectic design. In embroidery this took the form of an almost total reliance on Elizabethan and Jacobean styles, particularly among amateur embroiderers. However, among professional embroiderers ideas were changing gradually and there was concern at the poor quality of design. The efforts of English individuals such as Mary Hogarth and Rebecca Crompton, Head of Embroidery at Croydon School of Art, to remedy this situation were to have an effect by the 1930s when stitchery was being used to enhance the design. In Scotland Louisa Chart, lecturer in embroidery at Edinburgh College of Art, was a great influence through her teaching and her involvement in the Modern Embroidery Society founded in 1921.

A new approach was introduced into Aberdeen by Dorothy Angus who was appointed teacher of embroidery in 1920. She had studied with Louisa Chart in Edinburgh from whom she received a training in the tradition of the Royal School of Needlework with a thorough grounding in technique and an emphasis on excellent

stitchery. On her arrival in Aberdeen Dorothy Angus immediately set about introducing a higher standard of stitchery, more interesting use of colour and a strong graphic design content. The results were richly patterned surfaces worked in a variety of 'tapestry, crewel and botany wools supplemented by hectically coloured penny balls of wool'.[7] For finer work Filoselles, Floss silks, soft cotton and mercerized twist threads were used. In contrast to the debased Jacobean designs which Dorothy Angus abhorred, her students were encouraged to produce lively linear designs relating stitch and ground fabric to produce a unified textural whole.

Kathleen studied design with James Hamilton who was a distinctive figure in his bright green, Harris tweed, plus four suit, mauve shirt and pink tie. He was a remarkable man, an original thinker, communicating his ideas in 'fanciful jargon'. He opened his students' eyes to the wider art world and to an awareness of scientific development, but above all to the importance of the basic qualities of design. He stressed individuality and his most damning criticism of any design was 'by the yard'.

Under his guidance the students produced large, decorative but highly disciplined charcoal drawings which were translated under Dorothy Angus's supervision with great imagination in the use of stitchery, colour and tone, into rich textile surfaces using coloured wools in evenweave fabric. Although large scale embroidery was done elsewhere in the early 1930s, most notably in Glasgow where Kathleen Mann (a former student of Rebecca Crompton) was head of the Embroidery Department, there is a distinctive, lively and expressive use of stitchery in the work done in Aberdeen which sets it apart, and

continued on page 26

6   The Forest 1930
A sampler worked while a student. Natural linen embroidered in a wide range of stitches in shades of grey, green, pink, yellow, mauve, purple and brown silks. The colours were originally vivid but are now much faded. $21\frac{3}{4} \times 9\frac{1}{2}$ (55.3 × 24)

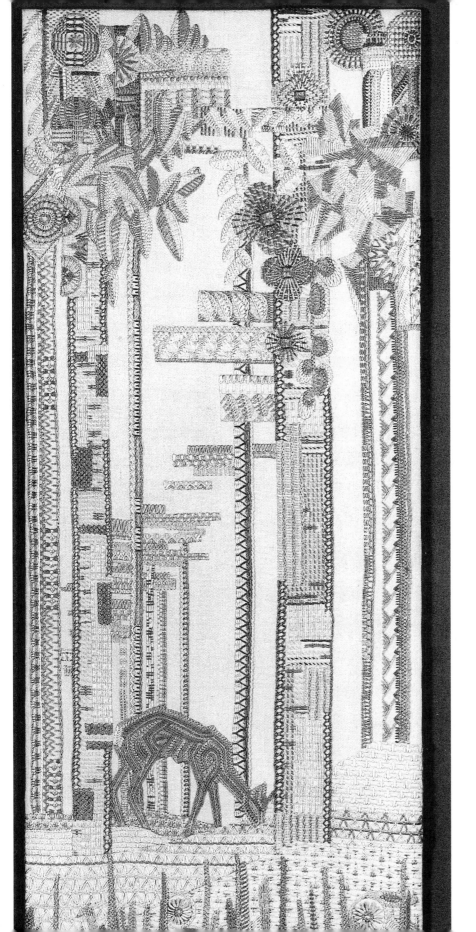

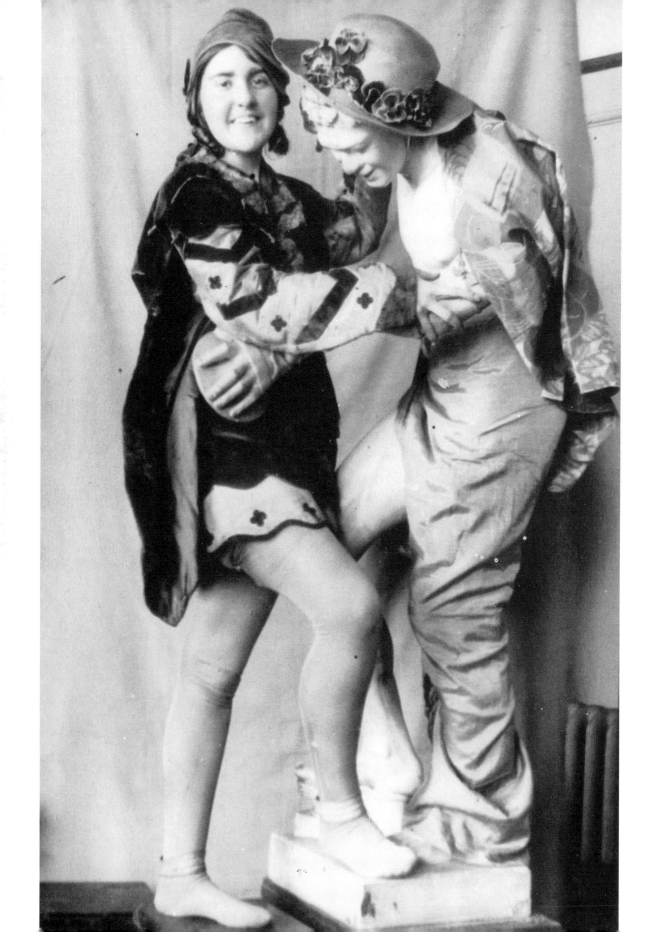

7   *Kathleen 'dancing' with one of the plaster casts in Grays School of Art*

8   *Dorothy Angus, extreme left dressed as an Egyptian, and Kathleen, third from the right, at a fancy dress evening in Aberdeen*

9   *Graduation ceremony, 1932. Kathleen is in the front row, third from the right*

10   *Diploma show, 1932, showing* Icarus *and immediately behind Kathleen,* The Fishwife

11   *Jacket, 1930–32*
*Black and green corded silk lined with pale
lime yellow rayon embroidered in vivid shades
of green, blue, orange and magenta cotton
and silk threads depicting stylized dragons.
The cuffs are cut in an interesting way*
Artist's collection

12   *Detail of the back of the jacket showing
the variety of stitches*

13

which Kathleen believes led the rest of Britain in the 1920s and early 30s.

Dorothy Angus was an inspiring teacher and a strong influence on her students. Kathleen remembers it was that on first impact 'what burst upon me as a revelation was the vast potential of stitchery. Here was an entirely new alphabet, the key to what I had been groping after all my life'.[8]

She used this new alphabet in a panel worked one vacation (*colour plate 1*). It was inspired by Eric Linklater's writings about *Sea Maas* (herring gulls) and illustrates a local saying 'keep your ain fish guts for your ain sea maas'. Roughly translated this means, look after your own. The panel depicts two seagulls, one swooping in to snatch the food regurgitated by the other. Her observations and interest in rendering water are translated into stitch formations which reinforce the line and sense of movement of the drawing.

13, 14, 15 and 16   Details of Kathleen's Diploma show

The expression of flight was extended in her Diploma piece *Icarus* (4) in which a great variety of stitches were used to suggest movement in the figure and the sea (5). The design of this large hanging with its sweeping forms, impression of speed and machine-like figure is typical of the 1930s, as in the use of wools on hessian. The strong greens, blues, orange and yellows in many tones are also typical and the broken black outline of the winged, streamlined figure enhances the dynamic design (*colour plate 2*).

In her fourth year, at home during the summer holiday, she worked a figure of a Fishwife, creating a three-dimensional appearance through her organisation of the stitchery which

14

15

she opened out or closed up to suggest the contours of the body. Dorothy Angus enthused over this piece and included it in an exhibition from where it was unfortunately lost. However, a miniature version of the figure appears in a later panel *Arbroath (colour plate 3)*.

Kathleen enjoyed Art School enormously, the students and staff were her kind of people. She could spend all her time doing the things she loved most, especially drawing. The school was small, there were twelve students in her year, which enabled everyone to see what everyone else was doing. Aberdeen has been an important educational centre since the founding of the university in the late sixteenth century. It also has medical and divinity schools and agricultural research centres. As one would expect it had a lively social life and was by no means a cultural backwater. The Art School was very near the Art Galleries and the students often went in to study

the paintings in their lunch hours. They were particularly keen on the work of Walter Sickert and Christopher Wood. His Majesties Theatre nearby had a constantly varied programme of plays, musical comedies and ballet – a seat in the Gods cost 6d (2½p). A few years later in the summer of 1934 more than one Ballet Company came from Russia to London and names such as Danilova and Massine became hallowed. There was also straightforward fun in fancy dress and theatrical entertainments and student 'rag' days (7 and 8).

Kathleen Whyte was a particularly successful student, winning the Founder's Prize as the best student in the second year of the general course, the Alexander Barker Prize as a result of the competition for third year students and in the fourth year won the Former Students Association Prize for her entry *The Fishwife*. In 1932 she was awarded a Diploma in Design and

16

Decorative Art, with distinction (*9*). A photograph (*10*) shows her standing beside her Diploma Show. She is wearing a jacket embroidered with stylized dragons (*11* and *12*). From other photographs (*13, 14, 15* and *16*) we have an idea of the graphic content of the course and the strength and quality of the design teaching.

17   Auchmithie *1932*
Natural linen ground with appliqué in yellow, pink, blue and ochre coloured linen with stitches in black, brown, orange, green and blue cotton threads. $17\frac{1}{4} \times 29$ *(44 × 73.6)*
Artist's collection

18   Postcard view of Auchmithie, near
Arbroath, in the 1930s

2 Early teaching 1932-48

After a year at Aberdeen Teacher Training College Kathleen became assistant art teacher at Frederick Street School in the East End of Aberdeen. She writes,

'I had no Art room and nothing that could be called equipment, but quantities of children, class after class of tough types, worthy citizens in embryo and poor little souls. I passed through the familiar stages of being scared of the whole lot, loathing lots of them and then coming to love them. I taught embroidery to all the girls, buying materials cheaply and collecting the cost in pennies per week. Art was very much the Cinderella of the curriculum but it never lacked champions, and both individuals and groups were constantly striving in many ways to raise the standard of work and to create better conditions.'[9]

Among other things the children made a large curtain depicting in felt appliqué the activities of the school. The boys drew and cut out some of these, the girls stitching them in place.

Leaving Frederick Street in 1940 she taught briefly at the Central Secondary School which because of wartime conditions was sharing the Grammar School building. The curriculum had a strong mathematical bias and she was later rewarded by pupils remembering that the varied activities she introduced 'weren't at all like school'. In all her teaching she has tried to get the pupils 'to open up to life, to get away from the stereotyped things'.

Kathleen then went on to the Aberdeen High School for Girls where she taught young girls and took craft classes with the older ones. When asked if she would go to the High School she said 'If you give me a room and a sink I'd go anywhere'. 'Teaching there was great fun, the girls were so fresh with their ideas and so absorbed in their work.' They made large painted panels to which everyone could contribute, one was of families blackberrying, another depicted Gulliver with lots of Lilliputians.

As well as teaching children she taught adults in the Art School evening classes where later during the War she taught servicemen and women to do leather work. James Hamilton was opposed to 'thonging' and so they did saddle stitching, making suitcases from skivers mounted on linen blind as well as other useful articles. She also did occupational therapy work

continued on page 36

19   Rafu The Mulberry Gatherer *1936*
Gold Chinese silk with applied fabrics in green, blue and purple, embroidered with orange, pink, gold, turquoise, black and white silk and cotton threads. There are also small pieces of cloth of gold.
Unlike appliqué of the 1920s, which often had the edges turned under or worked in buttonhole stitch, the edges are frayed and secured with stab stitches which follow the colour and pattern of the design.
17 × 15 (43.2 × 38)
Miss Betty Whyte

20   Arbroath *1943, detail*
The fishergirl and fisherman are created by
surface darning

21   Arbroath *detail*
Mary's Fish Shop is embroidered on top of
the padded white flannel shell shape, but is
slightly distorted to give the impression that it
is within the curving interior of the shell

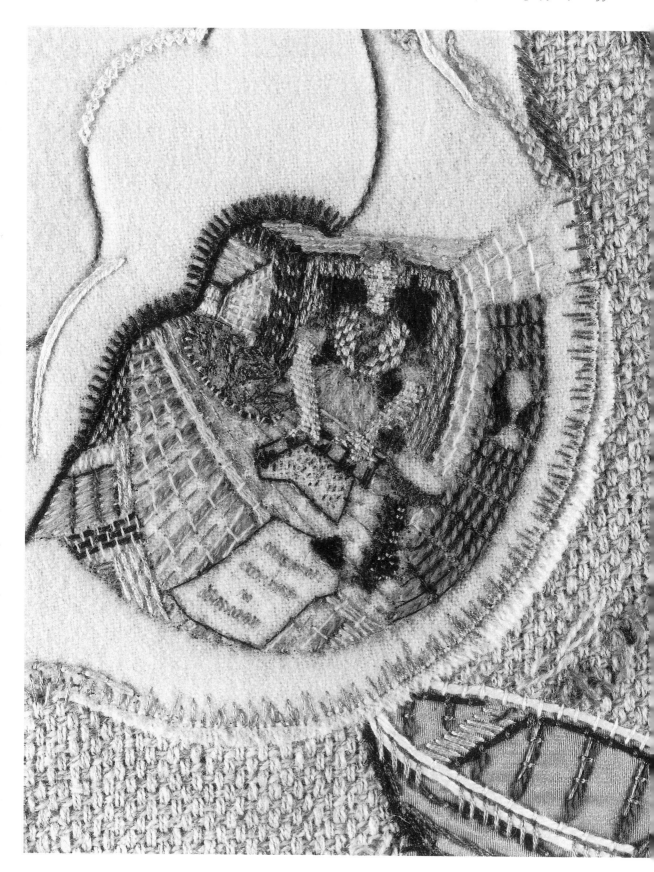

with hospital patients and in 1940 was made organiser of crafts in the newly formed youth clubs. One of the strengths of this varied teaching career was that she never had to enter a pupil for an art examination, therefore she was never inhibited by a rigid curriculum and was able to encourage individuality.

Throughout this time she produced her own work which she exhibited biannually with the Gray's School Former Pupils. She also exhibited a panel *The Mulbery Gatherer* (19), worked in 1936, at the Exhibition of British and Overseas Needlework, first in Aberdeen and then in the Academy of Needlework, Grosvenor Square, London. The idea for the panel came from a Chinese poem *A Ballad of the Mulberry Road*:

Her earrings are made of pearl
Her underskirt is of green pattern silk
Her overskirt is the same silk dyed in purple
When men look at Rafu
They stand, they put down their bundles
And twirl their moustaches
(Translated by Ezra Pound from a very early manuscript)

She also produced *Arbroath* (colour plate 3) using images from her early childhood when it was usual to see fisher girls with their creels and men at the shore (20). Mary's little fish shop was a special place (21). These she combined with designs based on three shells which she had been given, and added in the centre a mermaid with hair and tail of cloth of gold (22). This panel was originally exhibited as *The Catch* because 'fishermen never knew what they would find in their nets'. While she was a student Dorothy Angus had been commissioned to make an heraldic bedspread for Lord Glentanar, using cloth of gold and other sumptuous fabrics, which caused quite a stir among the students who helped to make it. Kathleen collected the tiny scraps and later used them in her mermaid. She also used pieces in the dress of *The Mulberry Gatherer*.

As well as continuing her embroidery she began to weave seriously. Kathleen taught herself to weave towards the end of her time at the School of Art when the department acquired

a loom. She wove material for a skirt and jacket which she later wore to her interview for her first teaching post at Frederick Street School. While visiting the Little Gallery in Sloane Square, London in the late 1930s she was impressed by the work of Ethel Mairet. In 1942, after reading her book *Handweaving in Education*, Kathleen wrote to Mrs Mairet and enclosed samples of her own work. She was invited to Ditchling. Ethel Mairet, although virtually self taught, was a highly respected craftswoman and a master in the use of vegetable dyes. She had set up a workshop, Gospels, at Ditchling in 1920. Initially her philosophy was very much in the Arts and Crafts tradition, but gradually in the late 1920s and 30s when she travelled widely in Europe and Scandinavia she modified her ideas as she accepted the necessity for craftsmen to design for industry. However, she was always most insistent about the maintenance of her exactingly high standards of design and workmanship. She was particularly enthusiastic about the modern hand loom weaving in Scandinavia and at Gospels began to experiment with new materials such as cellophane and rayon. This was an innovative period during which fabrics became much more textural. In the late 1930s Ethel Mairet began a series of courses for teachers who came in groups or, like Kathleen, as individuals. They were charged by the day for 'weaving and house'. She remembers it was a somewhat spartan existence and although Mrs Mairet was rather a difficult person Kathleen 'benefited from knowing this remarkable woman and appreciating the particular qualities with which she endowed hand weaving'.[10] On a return visit to Ditchling in 1943 together with other teachers and weaving apprentices she learned to spin and was encouraged to investigate a wider range of yarns (23).

Kathleen had started making her own clothes in the mid 1920s and in the early 1940s, because of wartime restrictions, she began weaving material for her mother, sister and friends, creating the fabric to suit the personality of the wearer (colour plate 4).

'Somehow in those days of scarcity and

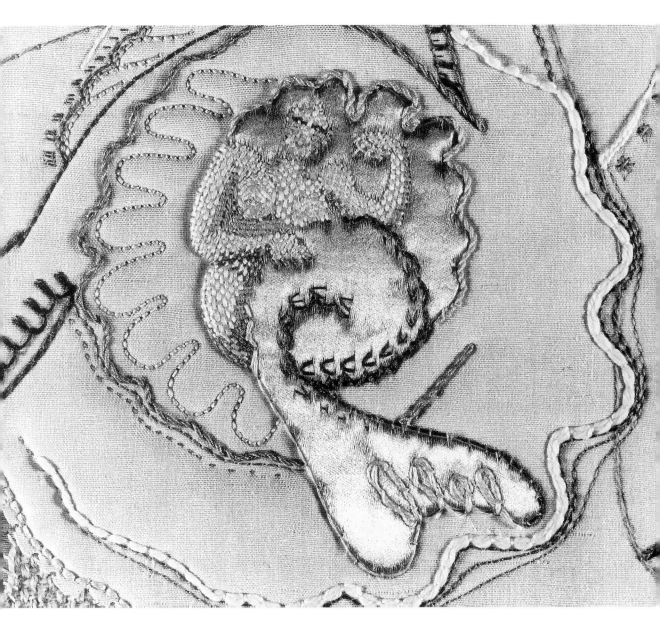

22   Arbroath *detail*
The figure of the mermaid is formed by
darning into the padded cloth of gold left
plain to form her tail and hair, which is edged
with a couched, twisted cord

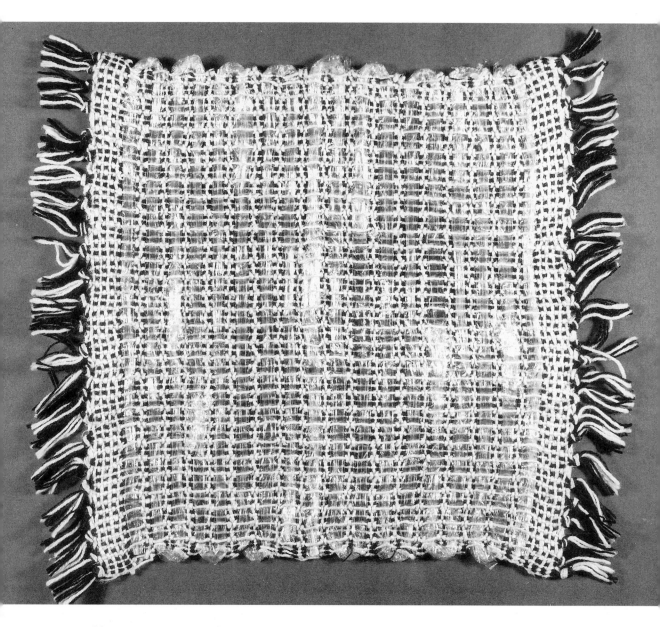

23   *Table mat, 1942*
An experimental piece of uncoloured
cellophane woven on a spaced black and
white cotton warp. Made by Kathleen at
Gospels, Ditchling. A similar but larger scale
fabric on a jute warp was woven as a wall
hanging, or complete wall covering by Ethel
Mairet. 9 × 11 (23 × 29.2)
Artist's collection

24   *Letters from Ethel Mairet written on her*
distinctive bright yellow stationery

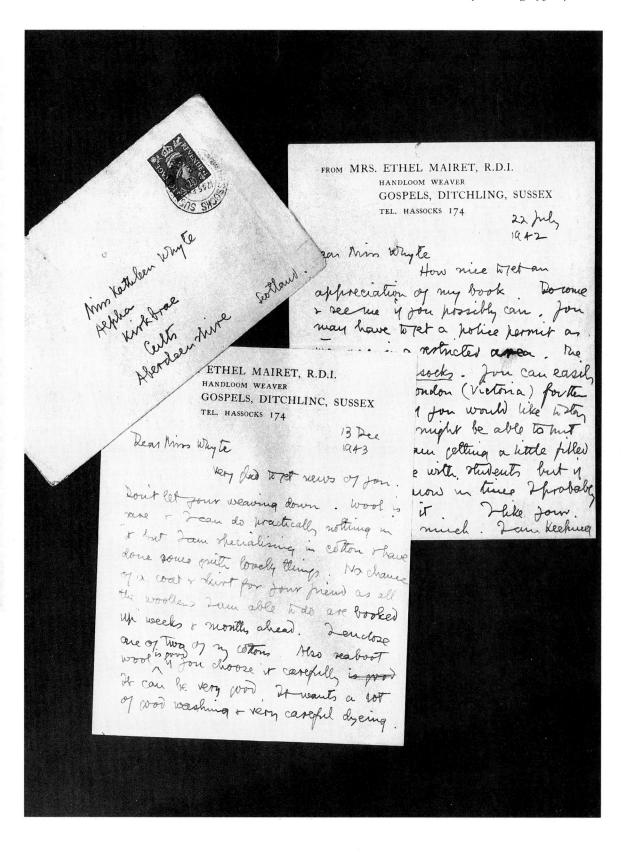

FROM MRS. ETHEL MAIRET, R.D.I.
HANDLOOM WEAVER
GOSPELS, DITCHLING, SUSSEX
TEL. HASSOCKS 174

22 July
1942

Dear Miss Whyte

How nice to get an appreciation of my book. Do come & see me if you possibly can. You may have to get a police permit as this is in a restricted area. The ...socks. You can easily ...ondon (Victoria) for the ...1 you would like to stay ...might be able to put ...am getting a little filled ...e with students but if ...now in time I probably ...it. I like your ...much. I am keeping

ETHEL MAIRET, R.D.I.
HANDLOOM WEAVER
GOSPELS, DITCHLINC, SUSSEX
TEL. HASSOCKS 174

13 Dec
1943

Dear Miss Whyte

Very glad to get news of you. Don't let your weaving down. Wool is rare & I can do practically nothing in it but I am specialising in cotton & have done some quite lovely things. No chance of a coat & skirt for your friend as all the woollens I am able to do are booked up weeks & months ahead. I enclose one of two of my cottons. Also seaboot wool is good & if you choose it carefully is good. It can be very good. It wants a lot of wool washing & very careful dyeing.

Miss Kathleen Whyte
Alpha
Kirkbrae
Cults
Aberdeenshire   Scotland.

25   *Charcoal drawing of the snow covered landscape around her home in Cults, Aberdeenshire, 1947*

clothing coupons it was always possible to get odd lots of yarns, sometimes lovely wools from hand spinners and at the other end of the scale opened out rug yarns, and by ingenious colour and texture schemes to weave lengths of material for willing clients. It was fun creating for individuals and in this small weaving enterprise I was greatly helped by a friend who was a very good dressmaker in one of those special establishments known as Court Dressmakers. She was a perfectionist and I learned a great deal from her.'[11]

In December 1943 she wrote to Ethel Mairet enquiring about the purchase of fabric and yarn and received the following letter:

Dear Miss Whyte,

Very glad to get news of you. Don't let your weaving down. Wool is rare and I can do practically nothing in it but I am specialising in cotton and have done some quite lovely things. No chance of a coat and skirt for your friend as all the woollens I am able to do are booked up weeks and months ahead. I enclose one or two of my cottons. Also seaboot wool is good if you choose it carefully. It can be very good. It wants a lot of very good washing and very careful dyeing. Some of my things are showing in Edinburgh. See them if you can.

Best wishes and hope to see you south again.

Yours sincerely,

(Signed)

Ethel Mairet

See also plate 24

In 1948 on the advice of Mr D M Sutherland, Head of Gray's School of Art, and supported by Dorothy Angus, Kathleen successfully applied for the post of embroidery and weaving lecturer in the design and craft section of Glasgow School of Art. She took her diploma piece *Icarus*, the *Arbroath* panel and her weaving samples to the interview. In September she succeeded in her resolve, formed while a student, and began to teach embroidery in an art school.

3 Glasgow: the embroidery revival in the post-war years

During the war Glasgow School of Art had functioned with fewer students and reduced number of courses and had shared accommodation with the British Red Cross Society and the Royal Air Force. Immediately after the war there was an enormous influx of students, including many ex-servicemen and women. The Governors and staff set about reintroducing craft subjects and a reorientation of the Design Department to meet the changing conditions in the field of industrial design. There were several newly appointed lecturers and a wave of enthusiasm ran through the new members of staff. It was a period of much discussion and there was a strong feeling of unity which was very heartwarming and uplifting, yet despite this it was a difficult time for Kathleen. She found that the standards of embroidery in the department had declined since the 1930s.

Agnes McCredie, her predecessor, had been in charge of the department since Kathleen Mann retired from full time teaching in 1934. Despite difficult wartime conditions she had introduced weaving and in 1948 Miss McCredie resigned to devote her time to the craft. As her interest in weaving had developed the subject assumed an equal footing with embroidery and the teaching of embroidery had stagnated. During this time the diploma students always completed some domestic articles and an ecclesiastical panel. These decorative panels were not innovative interpretations of religious ideas, nor were they expressed in traditional goldwork, but were straightforward pictorial illustrations of Old Testament themes. Kathleen immediately set about gradually changing and improving the course content.

At the same time as she was beginning to make improvements at the School of Art the Needlework Development Scheme was becoming much more active and was beginning to make an impact on a wider public. The NDS was founded in 1934 to raise the standard of embroidery design and to encourage a greater public interest in embroidery. It was instituted by J & P Coats in co-operation with the four Scottish Art Schools who organised the acquisition of well designed examples of British and foreign embroideries. Dorothy Angus, James Hamilton and Louisa Chart were responsible for the British and Irish sections, Kathleen Mann for the Italian and later Agnes McCredie was also involved. The collections were to be used by the embroidery departments and, later, also by training colleges, schools and other institutions. There were regular series of exhibitions, the first of which was organised by Louisa Chart in 1935, and lectures by visiting experts. The earliest series of lectures was given by Rebecca Crompton in 1937 when she visited Aberdeen, Dundee, Edinburgh and Glasgow. Although there was great interest in these lectures Rebecca Crompton never had the same widespread influence in Scotland that she enjoyed in England. The most profound impact of the NDS was caused by the beautifully designed examples of modern European and

26　*Spinning and Weaving Course, Jordanhill
College of Education, Glasgow 1948.
Margaret Clarke (later Kathleen's first full-
time assistant) carding, sits next to Kathleen
at the spinning wheel, watched by Emmeline
Thomson, the course organizer, immediately
behind*

Scandinavian work.

The Scheme had been in abeyance since
October 1939 and its reorganisation was dis-
cussed in March 1945 at the annual conference of
the four Central Art Institutions. An advisory
committee was set up consisting of representa-
tives of the Ministry of Education, the Scottish
Education Department and the Victoria and
Albert Museum. J & P Coats became responsible
for the maintenance of the collection, except for
some examples which became the property of the
Art Schools. Embroidery experts were appointed
for limited periods to ensure a vitality of approach and as wide a scope as possible in the
rapidly developing discipline. In 1946 Miss E K
Kohler was appointed as embroidery expert and
in 1948 she was succeeded by Miss Ulla Kockum
from Stockholm, whose arrival in Glasgow
coincided with that of Kathleen Whyte.

In August 1948, before taking up her post in
Glasgow, Kathleen taught spinning and weaving
on a course at Jordanhill College of Education
(26). This was the first of a series of three courses
organised by Emmeline Thomson, the Arts and
Crafts Adviser for the Scottish Leadership Training Association. One of the talks was given by
Ulla Kockum with whom Kathleen had become
friends. Immediately after the war, when travel

27   *Diploma show of Jack Lindsay, an interior design student, showing the rug woven in the Embroidery and Weaving Department, Glasgow School of Art, 1950*

was again possible, Kathleen had gone to Sweden to visit weaving centres such as Gothenburg and Boros, as well as Stockholm, and was impressed by Swedish design. She later met many other Scandinavian weavers including Eva Antilla from Finland and returned several times to Scandinavia. Like Ethel Mairet, Kathleen formed a particular attachment to Finland

'where a feeling of quality, the old "real" feeling was present in their artefacts and one realized that designers were important people in the community'.[12]

During the 1950s Scandinavian design continued to be highly regarded. Although their folk tradition had suffered a decline through growing industrialisation in the late nineteenth century a few individuals, influenced by William Morris and the Arts and Crafts Movement, had effectively halted this decline. Through the efforts of the Föreningen Handarbetets Vänner (the Friends of Weaving and Needlework) and Hemslöjds (Home Craft Associations) design in the

Swedish crafts had evolved successfully and adapted to modern life and new standards of design and industry. Such matters were of concern in Britain where, although some progress had been made, design still lagged behind other European countries. There were frequent exhibitions of Scandinavian design throughout Britain, including Glasgow School of Art whose staff and students also visited Denmark. For example, in 1948 an exhibition of Danish embroidery was held and Mrs Gertie Wandel, President of the Haandarbejdets Fremme (the Danish Handworkers Guild) gave a lecture on the Scandinavian attitude to good design. This was part of a tour organised by the Needlework

Development Scheme and the British Council. In 1952 Ulla Kockum Øverengen completed the booklet *Embroideries of Sweden* in the Needlework Development Scheme.

It was against this lively background that Kathleen began her teaching in earnest. Initially she had no full-time assistant and as well as

28   *Cushion, designed for the Festival of Britain Exhibition by Robert Stuart, embroidered by Kathleen Whyte.*
Red linen with white cotton embroidery.
20 × 20 (50.8 × 50.8)
Royal Museums of Scotland

29   *Cushion, designed for the Festival of
Britain Exhibition by Robert Stewart,
embroidered by Kathleen Whyte.
Blue linen with white and coloured
embroidery in a design suggesting a firework
display. 19 × 21 (48 × 53.5)*
Glasgow School of Art

teaching first and second year students she had her own thirteen embroidery and weaving students, a few of whom sadly doubted her ability 'to get their diplomas for them'. Gradually she overcame their suspicion and introduced the students to as many different techniques as possible and to experimentally suitable designs for each technique. In 1950 she introduced machine embroidery and tapestry weaving on high warp looms. Her method was to introduce a new technique and then encourage the students to experiment with it, finding its limitations and possibilities. She would demonstrate only when it was absolutely necessary, when a student had completely lost the way, and even then Kathleen only intervened enough to allow the learning process to continue. By 1950 the course content had been totally revitalised despite the limitations imposed by the lack of equipment and the shortage of materials caused by rationing which was still in force.

The change brought about by the new teaching staff of the Design Department is recorded in the School's annual report for 1949–50, which notes that in view of the higher standard of work produced by the students than in previous years the Governors provided three extra scholarships for the Design and Craft Department, one of which was for Embroidery and Weaving.

The Design courses were constantly being improved and developed in the light of commercial demands and what was being done in other schools. The Director Mr D Percy Bliss sent Robert Stewart and Kathleen Whyte to visit several English art schools to assess the content of the new Dip AD courses. Later Kathleen was invited to serve on the Dip AD visiting panel as an expert in embroidery – this she did for three or four years visiting Birmingham, Manchester, Cardiff and Loughborough. Close co-operation developed between Robert Stewart, Henry Hellier, Leslie Auld and Kathleen Whyte, the members of the Design Department. Interior design students were taught to weave rugs and she remembers one student appearing in the department with a loom he had made strapped to his back, ready for his instruction. His efforts can be seen in illustration 27. The embroidery students were also taught other aspects of design.

'We did screen printing with Bob Stewart, printing in lengths and pieces which I combined with machine embroidery. In interior design we produced pieces of furniture. I designed a metal and glass table to display a machine embroidery runner and a lampshade with machine embroidery and a hand made base.'[13]

A full-time assistant for embroidery had been appointed to take charge of General Course embroidery and help in the department. Margaret Clarke was the first, later in 1960 Ann Hunter joined the staff.

1951 was an important year for students and staff. During February the Council of Industrial Design invited the Design and Craft Department to exhibit at the Rayon Centre, Grosvenor Square. This was the first time any Scottish Art School had held an exhibition in London. It was well received by the public and press. This was also the year of the Festival of Britain. In addition

30   Figure of Christ 1950. *Designed by Robert Stewart, worked by Kathleen Whyte. The background is of bright pink Thai silk embroidered in rough gold with sequins and silk and cotton threads.* $7\frac{1}{4} \times 5$ *(18.5 × 12.7)* Robert Stewart

to the main event on the South Bank, London, there were exhibitions in Belfast and Glasgow, and the Needlework Development Scheme organised a travelling embroidery exhibition as part of the celebrations. For this exhibition Robert Stewart designed the lettering for two cushions which were worked by Kathleen (28

and 29). The following year, 1952, she was asked to weave a length of material for the Enterprise Scotland Exhibition, held in Edinburgh.

By the mid 1950s the Design and Crafts Department was the largest in the School and the external assessors congratulated the staff on their close teamwork. The Director, commenting on the annual diploma show, said:

'Trade visitors to the three sections (Interior Design, Printed Textiles and Embroidery and Woven Textiles) were again emphatic that the old reproach against students' work being unprofessional and arty crafty does not apply in Glasgow.'[14]

Despite this co-operation between lecturers some embroidery students felt slightly isolated when in 1964, because of approaching demolition of the building in Renfrew Street, the departments of Graphics, Textiles and Embroid-

31 and 32   Students working in Glasgow School of Art Embroidery Department in Bath Street in the late 1960s

ery and Weaving had to be found homes outside the main complex. Embroidery and Weaving went to a house in Bath Street where they remained for five years. In spite of poor lighting and overcrowding much interesting work was produced there (31 and 32). In 1970 when the department moved into the newly constructed Newbery Tower and once again became part of the main school any feelings of isolation which students may have had were dispersed. Because they became more aware of the work being done, the move also helped to dispel the belief among some students in other departments that embroidery was trivial. Throughout her career

Kathleen has been very conscious of the status of embroidery and has worked hard to establish its status as a valid means of self expression.

In the early years at Glasgow her students did weaving, which with spinning and dyeing occupied half the students' time, third year students using table looms for pattern making and designing, the fourth year using various types of floor looms. In 1964 a full-time assistant for weaving was appointed, this in addition to a technical assistant who had been installed for some years was a great advantage. Between third and fourth years students spent three weeks at the Scottish College of Textiles in Galashiels. In the first year in 1949 Kathleen had done the course with the students. This course gave a good grounding in technique and an understanding of industrial processes. Although the weaving produced was not as technically complex as the student work today, nonetheless it was a sound basis from which they were encouraged to experiment. In the final year students produced three lengths of cloth; a coat length; a dress length and an upholstery fabric. They also produced various types of rugs and spun fleece which was used in various ways (*33, 34* and *35*).

In 1957 Marianne Straub was one of the external assessors, who while acclaiming the high standard of embroidery pointed out that, 'In weaving nothing like the same enterprise in being shown'.[15] Later in 1970 the appointment of Carol Jones gave a strong impetus to weaving.

33 Part of the Diploma Show, 1952
Showing a central display of jackets and skirts
made from woven lengths

34 Part of the Diploma Show with a variety
of woven fabrics

35   *Part of one student's Diploma Show,*
1953

Kathleen commenting on the changes taking place in embroidery wrote in the *Scottish Art Review* in 1958:

'Everything is in favour of good embroidery today – materials, colour and design – everything with the possible exception of time, but a surprisingly large number of people are making time to pursue this most absorbing craft. Exhibitions show, both by entries and attendances, that its popularity is growing, and that the standard of work is rising, while among embroideresses themselves there is a spirit of receptiveness and an eargerness to profit by professional criticism. All over the country groups of enthusiasts are meeting to share their knowledge and avail themselves of instruction. There are various reasons for this quickened interest. Embroidery flourishes in times of domestic prosperity and free intercourse among nations, and also when the beauty of her home is an important factor in every woman's life. In times of war or stringent economy ingenuity can have interesting results, as we well know, but the fact remains that a wealth of lovely materials, and the appropriate settings for her work, are two of the greatest incentives to the embroideress.

'Today as never before are we conscious of design in our homes, and aware of the effects of good colour, but an overemphasis on stream-lined and mass-produced articles tends to make us turn with relief to things made by hand. Foreign influence, particularly from Scandinavia which has of late years so noticeable laid its mark on furniture, textile and silver design, has also touched embroidery in this country to its decided advantage. This is particularly so in the domestic field where Danish and Swedish work displays such imaginative design and desirable simplicity.

'Influence may come from abroad but effort comes from within our midst, and we are now beginning to see the result of a long period of devoted effort by individual enthusiasts, and by schools of art and other organisations working for the betterment of embroidery.'[16]

58 Silver Cross *1973*
White mohair darned in heavy silks, rayons,
lurex and silver threads. 48 × 30 (122 × 76)
Scotch Whisky Association

59   *Sampler for* Silver Cross
Artist's collection

Lecturer for the Fortieth Anniversary of the Needlework and Textile Guild of Chicago. She also travelled to Tucson, Arizona. To illustrate these talks she prepared many stitch samplers (66) and at the end of the tour she was given a book containing mementos of her visit, including press cuttings reviewing her lectures which were enthusiastically received.

Kathleen Whyte has a gift for words and has written many articles on all aspects of embroidery and in 1963 prepared a leaflet *Embroidery with Unusual Materials* for the Embroiderers' Guild. Before going to America she had been invited by Thelma Nye of Batsford to write a book. The result was *Design in Embroidery* published in 1969. Although she found it much

more difficult to write this book than to do embroidery, with her usual thoroughness and attention to detail (she also designed the layout), she succeeded in producing a work which is a comprehensive and complete design course. It contains the essence of her philosophy of embroidery and approach to teaching. It has been accepted as a seminal work on design in countries as far away as America and New Zealand, and its importance to the discipline of embroidery cannot be overstated.

In 1974 she retired from teaching at Glasgow School of Art and to mark the occasion a dinner was held and large lithographic portraits of her were produced. As a mark of the high regard in which she was held the Royal Glasgow Institute of the Fine Arts included a retrospective exhibition of her work, plus over forty embroideries by her former students, in their annual exhibition.

60   Fire Pond 1 *1971*
Brown and black tweed background
embroidered with black, grey, green, blue,
orange and yellow wools, green, blue, yellow
and brown cotton threads. 15 × 18 (38 × 46)
Mr John Wallace

61   Fire Pond 2 1973
*Natural silk with irridescent threads and gun
metal leather. 8¼ × 12 (12 × 30.5)*
*The designs for Fire Ponds 1 and 2 were
suggested by the pond at Culzean Castle,
Ayrshire which was installed as a ready
supply of water in case of fire.*
National Gallery of Victoria, Australia

62   White Waves 1968
*The design is built up in white tissue paper on
brown paper and is based on a chalk sketch.
The finished panel is of orange Donegal
hopsack embroidered with a variety of white
yarns including rough spun linen and nylon
knitting yarn in rosette chain, crested chain
and cable chain stitches. 45 × 15 (114 × 38)*
Embroiderers' Guild

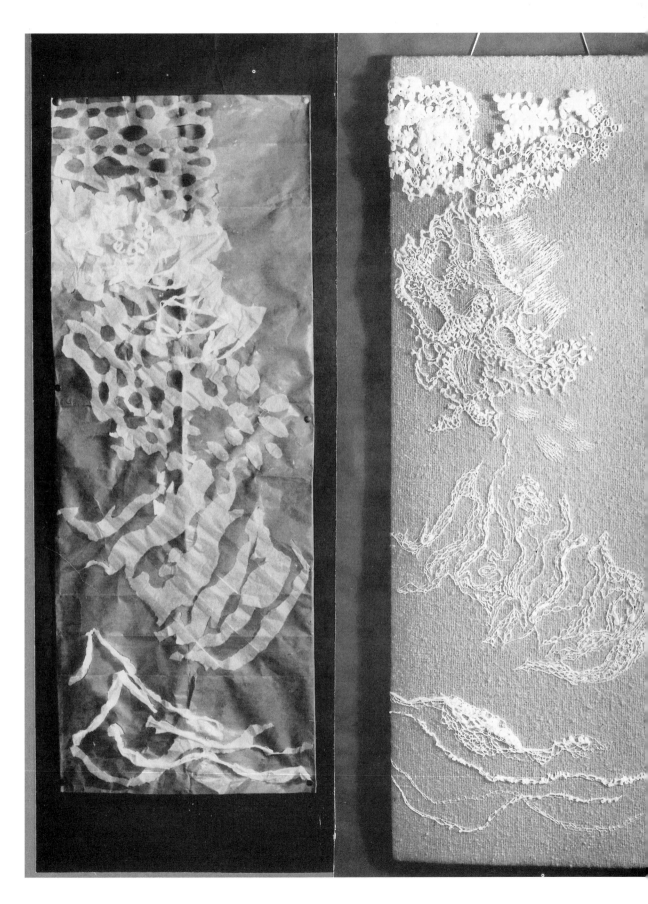

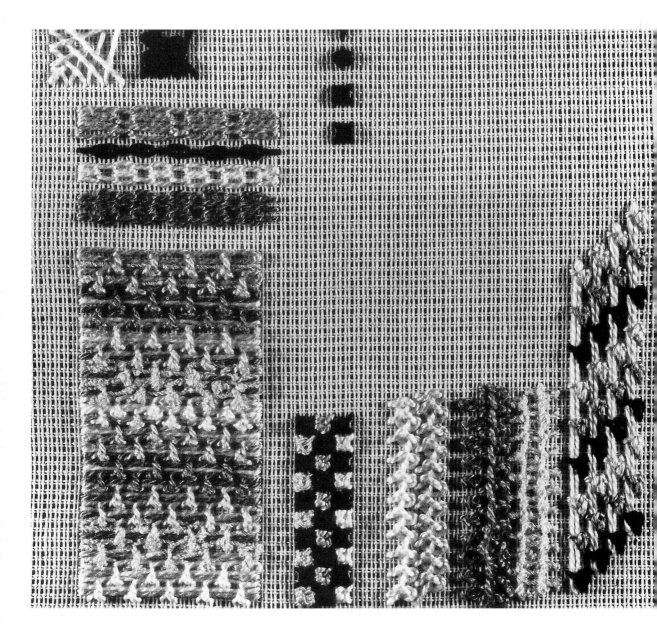

63 *Stitch sampler, 1967*
Grey and black wool, silver lurex and white
cotton worked in rows of sheaf stitch with
groups of three colours to create a pattern
Artist's collection

64 *Stitch sampler, 1967*
Double canvas with pale yellow and bright
yellow, two tones of grey, and black cotton
threads in rosette chain, cable chain and
various knot stitches
Artist's collection

65   Sampler, early 1970s
Darning and surface darning
Artist's collection

66   Sampler, 1967
Two patterns for borders, canvas with wools,
nylon, rayon, silver knitting yarn and confetti
chenille
Artist's collection

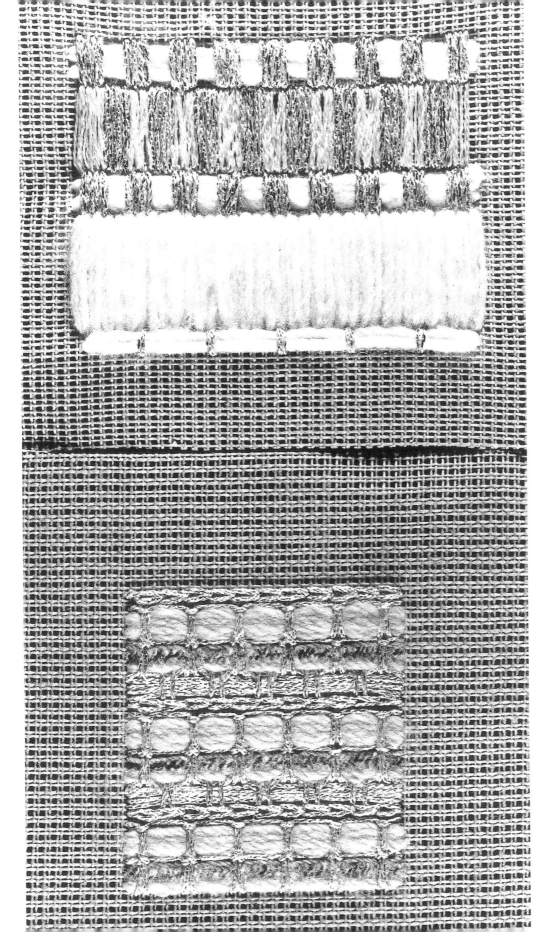

67 *Linen sampler, 1967*
Worked as an illustration for Design in
Embroidery *to show the quality and
behaviour of various linen yarns, thick rough
spun to hard waxed threads on linen paper*
Artist's collection

68 Parlour Game *1973*
*A manipulative embroidery in a succession of
curving shapes which moved on perspex rods
and could be reorganised to create a number
of linear patterns. Kathleen considered this
piece unsatisfactory and dismantled it*

6 Commissions

Since the 1920s there has been an increasing attempt to beautify the churches of the Church of Scotland and in 1934 an Advisory Committee, which included several distinguished artists and architects, was set up to advise congregations. It was stressed that designs should be in keeping with the doctrines of the Church as well as having aesthetic appeal. Symbolism was considered important, but no representation of the human figure was allowed. Most of the crafts were acceptable, although painting was not considered appropriate. The main vehicles for embroidery are pupit falls and communion cloths to cover the Communion Table, which takes the place of an altar. By the 1950s there was greater press interest and public awareness in this development and since this time ecclesiastical embroidery has played a large part in Kathleen's career.

She enjoys the challenge and discipline of designing for different architectural settings, allowing the spatial proportions, the colour, the structural materials and the general atmosphere to become a contributing factor in the final design. She finds it particularly satisfying and stimulating to work for other people, and enjoys solving the problem of conveying the message through the design in a way which satisfies her clients' demands. It also provides a marvellous opportunity to produce embroidery as a focus for many people's attention and contemplation through the use of symbolism. Symbolism is a basic element of ecclesiastical art which conveys spiritual beliefs and concepts through a timeless visual language which she uses to great effect. She has frequently used the simple yet powerful symbol of a cross within a circle as a starting point as she believes that this provides an infinite variety of opportunities.

One of her earliest commissions in 1952 was a plain linen communion cloth on which she embroidered a circular crown of thorns design using simple stitchery (69). This was quickly followed by a vivid pulpit fall for St Martin's Church in Port Glasgow (70). This piece was inspired by primitive jewellery which suggested the idea of bright silk inserts in rough gold. The metal threads are couched in varying directions to create facets of light and shade. The design of a cross contained within a circle representing the elements, humanity and animal and plant life is worked on a long strip of scarlet handwoven silk with a horizontal bar of gold near the foot. This pulpit fall with its beautifully simple and carefully proportioned design of gold symbols supplies a vital streak of colour and a focal point in a simple modern church.

In a pulpit fall for St Brendan's Church, Bute (71) Kathleen was asked to produce a design with a Scottish flavour. Again she used a circular

69 *Communion cloth, 1952*
White linen embroidered in natural tones ranging from white to brown
Shawlands Old Parish Church, Glasgow

70   Creation, *pulpit fall, 1959, detail*
Red handwoven ecclesiastical silk with laid
gold. 34 × 18 (86.2 × 45.7)
St Martin's Church, Port Glasgow

71   Targe, *pulpit fall, 1960*
Natural silk background with circular targe in
tones of pink and red silk and chiffon, with
pale gold kid
St Brendan's Church, Bute

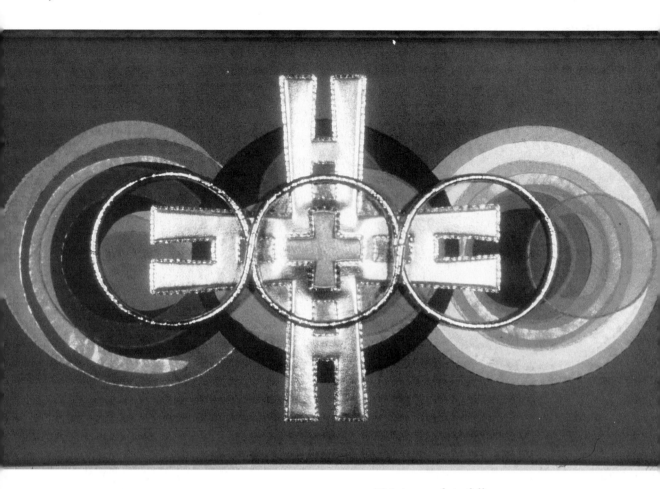

motif, this time based on a targe – a small, round, leather covered wooden shield frequently decorated with metal bosses which is traditionally associated with the Highlands. The cross of pale gold kid is set against the suggestion of a St Andrew's cross and contained within a ring of pairs of small circles alternating with single circles, some like stylized thistles. These small circles and the whole piece have something of the splendour of a Cairngorm brooch, while at the same time suggesting the ancient Celtic culture and origin of the Church in Scotland.

On another occasion the same motif of circles and a cross was repeated to express the idea of the Trinity in which three ajoining, three dimensional circles are linked by a cross of gold kid. Behind are appliquéd coloured circles which create depth and movement emphasizing the static, immutable Trinity (72). The bold use of

72 Trinity, *pulpit fall, 1973*
Vivid red silk background with circles in tones of red, pink, orange and purple silk and chiffon with gold kid
Cathcart South Church, Glasgow

73 Dove, *pulpit fall, early 1950s*
Bright green velour with pale gold cross on a white circle. The dove is white and silver, padded and richly decorated with sequins
Church of Hamilton Bardrainney, Port Glasgow

74   Holy Spirit, *pulpit fall, 1973*
Pink and orange checked silk background,
dove is of padded white silks and the building
is of gold leathers and metal threads.
18 × 14 (46 × 35.5)
Old Parish Church, Gourock

75   Dove and Rainbow, *pulpit fall, 1982*
Fawn silk with raised and padded dove in
white with subtle tones of mauve and gold
metallic organzas and fine silver leathers. The
rainbow is in vivid colours. 30¼× 20½ (77 × 52)
Westerton Church, Bearsden

shapes creates a simple statement which can be
clearly read from any part of the church. A
dramatic effect is created by the highlights of the
smooth areas of gold kid set against the rich red
of the background.

Kathleen has used the circle (symbol of sun,
life and eternity) together with a dove (symbol of
the Holy Spirit and peace) in three pulpit falls,
the first of which was worked in 1950 (73). In the
second (74) Christian symbols and suggestions of
ancient Scottish history combine to convey the
subject of the Holy Spirit breaking through the
bounds of the building of the church. The
padded dove is seen against an opened circle like
the ground plan of a Pictish wheelhouse which is
an integral part of the symbolic building. The
building is worked in squares and rectangles of
gold and copper kid with Jap gold which relates
to the chequered pink and orange background.
The richness of the technique not only adds to
the impact at a distance but allows embroidery
added interest when seen closely. Choice of

colour too is important, not only because of its liturgical significance but also because it speaks directly to the emotions of the viewer. The latest of the dove pulpit falls (75) was made in 1982 and depicts the dove carrying olive leaves with a semi-circular rainbow behind.

The most striking and impressive of all her ecclesiastical embroideries, which demonstrates her ingenuity so clearly, is the Mayfield Cloth, made as the front of a communion table cover and as the focal point for a reconstructed church in Edinburgh which had been largely destroyed by fire (76). Describing this commission she wrote:

'Two ideas eventually came together to determine the form of the design. I had for some time wanted to use the symbol of the Hand of God in a church embroidery, and as I stood looking at the bare chancel I sensed I must try to create the feeling of people coming together. So the idea grew in my mind – converging on the Hand of God. This in turn linked itself to an interest in finding ways in which to express movement within design and finally an architectural photograph of an arrangement of vertical stone slabs provided the basic idea on which to work. After experimenting with various design arrangements, a wing-like structure with an inward thrusting movement eventually took shape and can be seen in the photograph as the upper layer of the design on either side. This by itself, however, looked too small and thin, so part of it was enlarged considerably and placed to appear beneath the original formation, giving greater weight and density within the design as a whole, as well as a feeling of thronging achieved by overlapping the two divergent line formations. Symmetrical repetition of the whole structure then created two vanishing points assuring a strong thrust towards the centre where the hand would find its place.

'As I worked to adjust this bare scaffolding of line formation I saw it clothed in colour, a mosaic of moving gradations and cross-currents leading the eye up and round and into the centre and also providing the work with liveliness and sparkle.

'For the background I chose a cool, pale golden putty shade of material and from more than sixty colours of silks and rayons I organised a palette of tonal ranges comprising darkest purples, maroons and bronze browns, copper shades, flame, scarlet, orange and salmon pinks, also cool mauves and ice pinks, cream and off white, buffs, lemon yellows and gold colours. To these were added metallic fabrics and leathers as well as chiffons and other transparencies which were useful for overlaying other materials and thus creating further subtle shades when necessary.

'A form of traditional patchwork seemed to offer the best method of obtaining juxtaposition of colour with accuracy of shape. First of all the larger lower part of the design was traced on to *Vilene* which was then cut out to form the necessary foundation for the patches and was retained in the finished work. Patches were then sewn together to form convenient areas, leaving gaps where the ground colour was intended to show and these areas were in turn hemmed in position on the background material. Where the lower part of the design was complete the upper wing-like formations were made in a similar way, superimposed and sewn in place. Lastly additional shapes of colour and gold leathers were inserted to complete the 'converging' form. All the work was carried out without stretching the background. The gold hand was made separately on a foundation of net stretched on a frame. The shape of the hand was cut out of pelmet *Vilene*, padded with layers of felt to create a bas-relief and covered with gold plastic material. The net was then cut away and the hand arranged to emerge from overlapping circles denoting infinity and eternity. The small

76 *Communion cloth, 1972*
Gold putty coloured background with over sixty colours in silks, rayons, metallic fabrics, leathers, chiffons and other transparent fabrics. 36 × 60 (91 × 152.4)
Mayfield Church, Edinburgh

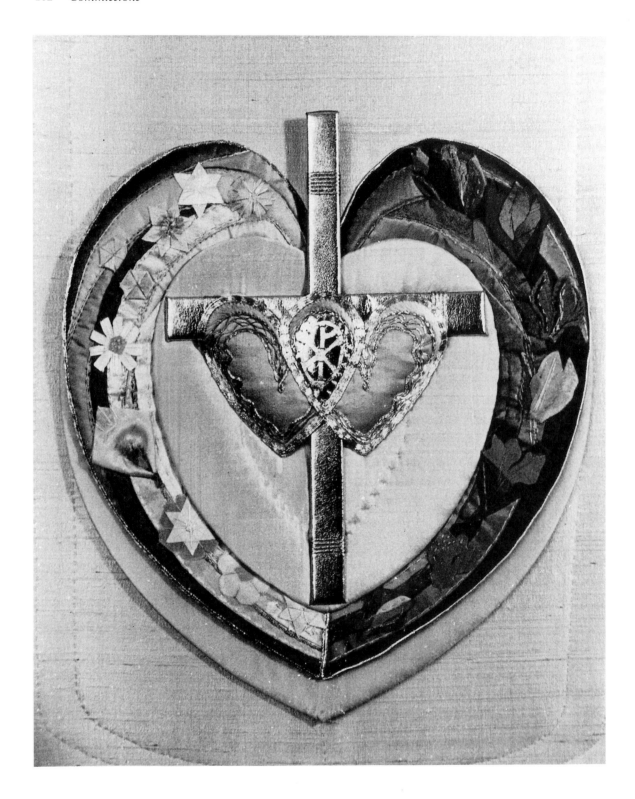

cross lying in the palm is mounted on a scarlet circle and has a Celtic appearance.

'The natural feeling of the hand and the abstract nature of the 'convergence', although a seeming inversion of the usual concept is intentional to create dramatic tension.'[26]

A more intimate commission was that for a pulpit fall commemorating her former teacher and friend Dorothy Angus and her sister-in-law Margaret (77). Colour and floral motifs were used to represent the sisters, purples and blues for Dorothy, gold and yellow for Margaret. The overall shape is a heart with a central cross. Superimposed on the cross is a double heart motif in which the central overlapping section contains a Chi Rho. This double heart motif is like the popular Luckenbooth brooches which were worn in Scotland during the eighteenth and nineteenth centuries as tokens of love. It expresses affection and dignity in an appropriate tribute to her teacher who was such an inspiration.

Another commemorative piece is the figure panel which hangs in the vestibule of Netherlee Church whose minister, the Rev Stanley Mair, it commemorates (78). It depicts triumph and hope in the figure taken from St John's vision in the Book of Revelation. The head is made in a bas relief technique against a bright spectrum of patched silk in the form of a cupola, the garment

77   *Commemorative pulpit fall 1980*
White silk background with a variety of fabrics in low relief in tones of blue and purple on the right, gold and yellow on the left, with gold kid. $21\frac{3}{4} \times 19\frac{1}{4} (55 \times 49)$
Stenton Church, Midlothian

78   Netherlee Figure *1978*
Indian and Thai silks in orange, gold and red with some purple and rainbow colours, and gold leathers, using patchwork and quilting. The face has been built up in layers of gold leather. $65 \times 22\frac{1}{2} (165 \times 57)$
Netherlee Church, Glasgow

is quilted with a symbolic design based on the plan of a medieval church. The breast plate is of woven gold leathers and incorporates a white stone. Several motifs around the figure relate to Stanley Mair's life: the Chinese sign of Yin and Yang representing his birth and early life in China; the crown of King's College Aberdeen from which he graduated; a Cinthe for his war service with the Chindits in Burma; a heart and two rings for his married life and the figure holds a trumpet and scroll with the words *Logos Dei Euntes Ergo Docete Gloria, Benedicte* (go therefore and teach) which represent his ministry.

Commissions have not been limited to those for the church. In August 1966 Queen Elizabeth and the Queen Mother performed the opening ceremony of the Tay Road Bridge and a new opportunity presented itself. A stole was chosen by her Majesty from several suggested gifts and it was commissioned by the Tay Road Bridge Joint Board through the Scottish Craft Centre, of which Kathleen is a founder member (79, 80 and 81).

'The stole itself was pure silk, handwoven in cream and gold by Ursula Brock of Malden, Essex. It was a beautiful article and proved to be an interesting background on which to work. When I was asked to do the embroidery I was presented with the intriguing idea of creating a design to feature a quantity of pearls from the River Tay. These proved to be very lovely. They were supplied by a jeweller in Perth who made the final selection of forty pearls and had them pierced for sewing. They ranged in size from small seeds to boutons of three-eights of an inch [9.5mm] diameter, and the colours and lustres varied from clear pinks through all the pearl shades to gold and deep mauve. Some were irregular in form which added to their interest.

79   *Her Majesty, Queen Elizabeth,*
The Queen Mother, 1966
(*Courtesy the* Dundee Courier)

80   *Kathleen with the completed Tay Bridge Stole, 1966*
(*Courtesy the* Dundee Courier)

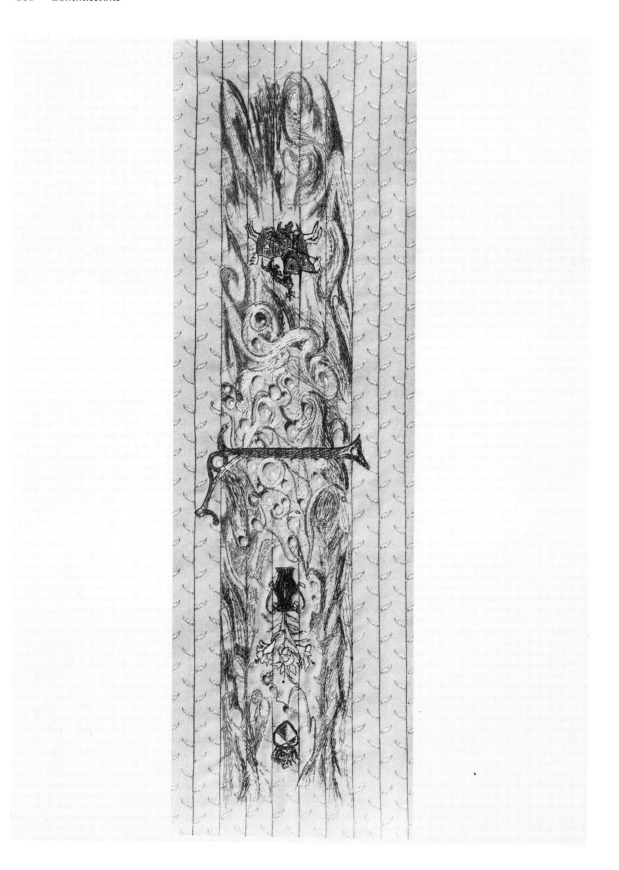

◀81　*Detail of the embroidered stole*

82　Storks Fly in the Dawn *1971*
Background is of furnishing fabric, orange-red
at the top, with deeper red and brown at the
bottom. 24 × 72 (61 × 183)
Queen Mother Hospital, Glasgow

The intention throughout was to make something charmingly wearable and my first impression was of a simple gold tissue-like river, spanned by a bridge which I had heard was very straight. When, however, I was shown the bridge designer's plans I was delighted to discover that, if they were scaled right down, the bridge with its approach road systems at either end would have quite the appearance of a Celtic clasp which could be worked in Japanese gold with pearls inset for roundabouts. All the other pearls I imagined grouped together forming the highlight of the embroidery, in a white swirling cascade flowing under the bridge. It was fortunate that the three symbolic devices which had to be included in the design – a crowned heart for Angus, a pot of lilies for Dundee and a knight on a charger for Fife – were such pleasant shapes and could be used agreeably together. Colour throughout the work was planned mainly in gold and white as a foil to the subtle tints of the pearls – the heart only being a deep oyster mauve, exactly the shade of the deepest pearl, and the horse's trappings a brownish pink allied to gold, while the lilies could stand in a silver pot.

'. . . Various white silks in split and stem stitches were used in working the swirl of water which serves as a background to the pearls and here of course it was necessary to obliterate the vertical lines of the pattern; but what may not be so obvious is the use made of the arcs suggested by the leaf pattern. Many of these arabesques are based on these curves, thus keeping the scale of this part of the design consistent with the background. The pearls themselves were of course entirely fascinating to handle and organise, but since no single pearl could be sewn in position until all others had been carefully returned to their box it became necessary to make a plan – their relative positions were sketched and numbered on a tracing and the pearls rethreaded on to their original fine wire according to the numbers. Thus each one as required could be located and fixed in position. It was possible to use a bead needle for all except the very small seed pearls: these were secured by one strand of silk waxed to a fine point to pass through the hole. This proved to be time-consuming. The actual time spent in working the stole was sixty-five hours.

'In a commission such as this, where time is neat and where there are so many given factors, problems become very clearly defined. This can add to the fascination and call forth a particular response from the embroiderer. I found the whole project most delightful, and was overjoyed that embroidery should be chosen for such an important presentation.'[27]

Perhaps the most straightforward, realistic and intuitive design was the result of a commission by a young architect as an expression of gratitude to the Queen Mother Hospital for Mothers and Babies in Glasgow (82). (This was one of two panels, the other was designed and made by her former student and colleague Hannah Frew Paterson.)

'The panel was to be sited at the entrance to the Special Care Unit to be seen by anyone waiting to enter this area where tiny lives are saved and nurtured. I came to think of this design as something to divert or momentarily arrest the attention of expectant or anxious young fathers, something gay, light-hearted and calm. The size was decided at six feet by two feet [183 cm × 61 cm] and rather surprisingly the subject "storks" was suggested to me. This at first caused some dismay, then I thought "why not?" and why not go for realism and make something very easy to look at. . . .

'The storks were made of an off white furnishing material, satin side and reverse side, also white pvc and dark maroon pvc for beaks and legs. The shapes were quilted on the sewing machine and stuffed from the back as in Italian quilting, then assembled with as much overlapping as possible. The area of pattern between the two birds which denotes the rays of the rising sun and also establishes a continuity of flying and flapping was developed from a drawing of feathers greatly magnified. The linear part is built up in thick shaded bouclé wools and folds of silk materials in rich reds and purples while "flags" are made of golds and copper colours. An embryo chick in a golden eggshell is caught between overlapping discs within the sun which is pure golden yellow. The larger of the babies is pale gold and the other one bronze in colour. They sit among cut out cotton daisies.'[28]

In all her commissioned work one is struck by the ingenuity and variety with which she expresses traditional ideas. While she was a student Dorothy Angus commented on this ability, pointing out that any ideas she had given Kathleen were carried far beyond what she imagined possible. Since then she has continued to develop every idea from the foundations rather than being guided by current theories of design. She has also encouraged this trait in her students, many of whom have undertaken both secular and ecclesiastical commissions.

The development of ecclesiastical embroidery has of course not been confined to Scotland and there are many notable exponents of this branch of embroidery. This growth of interest has resulted in several exhibitions which although depriving the works of their original architectural settings have allowed them to be seen by a wider public. In 1968 an Exhibition of New Ecclesiastical Embroidery was held in the crypt of St Paul's Cathedral, London. One reviewer noted that 'The Scottish works on show are very fine, distinguished by their restraint and an effective if surprising combination of weight and delicacy'.[29] Kathleen exhibited a pulpit fall *Burning Bush* (83) commissioned for Allan Park Church, Stirling and *The Last Supper* (84) which another reviewer described as 'having something of the sensitive delicacy of a Byzantine ivory carving. The chromatic scale of subtle browns and purples which draws the eye along the row of twelve Disciples is particularly good.'[30] This small panel was not a commission and was gifted to the Royal Scottish Museum, Edinburgh. Later, in 1976, Kathleen Whyte exhibited another pulpit fall (85) in the Exhibition of Contemporary Ecclesiastical Embroidery at Hereford Cathedral.

83   Burning bush, *pulpit fall, 1964*
Strong green-gold background with flame coloured fabrics and stitchery, with gold kid.
30 × 22 (76 × 56)
Allan Park Church, Stirling

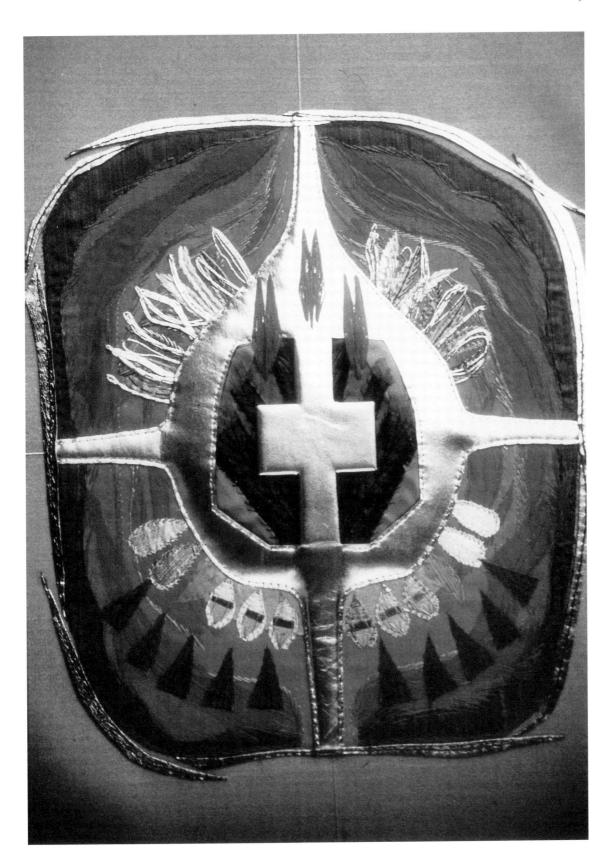

The Tay Bridge Stole has also been seen by the general public in 1968, in the 'Skill' Exhibition which was staged by the Institute of Directors, The Crafts Centre of Great Britain and the Scottish Craft Centre. It was held in Goldsmiths' Hall, London, before travelling to Glasgow. The stole was shown again in 1987 in a retrospective exhibition of her work, organized by the Scottish Branches of the Embroiderers' Guild and held in Edinburgh College of Art.

84   The Last Supper *1957*
Padded purple silk with laid gold, appliqué and silk embroidery.
The whole motif is a truncated cross with a symbolic figure of Christ, Judas with a grasping hand is at the extreme right. 9 × 16 (23 × 40.7)
Royal Museums of Scotland

85   Arms of Gourock, *pulpit fall, 1976*
Commemorative pulpit fall presented by the Town Council on the occasion of the change in local government.
Brick red background with strong heraldic colours and a silver leather boat representing the church. 20 × 14 (51 × 35.7)
Old Parish Church, Gourock

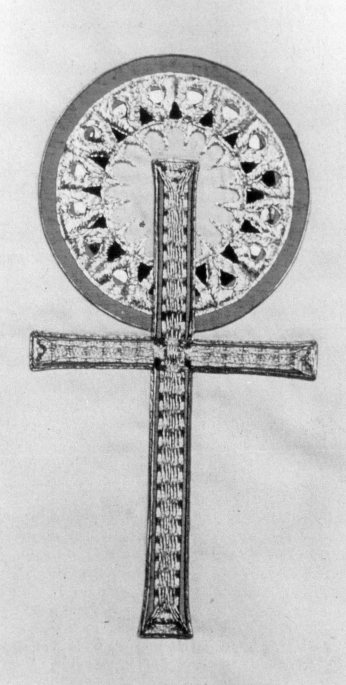

86 *Pulpit fall, early 1950s*
White silk background with laid gold in
various tones and a pale olive green circle
Fernhill and Cathkin Church, Glasgow

87 *Pulpit fall, 1981*
Warm golden brown furnishing fabric with
silks and rayons in blue, purple, red, orange,
yellow and white with silver leather and silver
metal thread.
The vertical of the cross represents the steel
works where many of the expatriot Scots who
make up the congregation are employed
Church of Scotland, Corby, Northampton

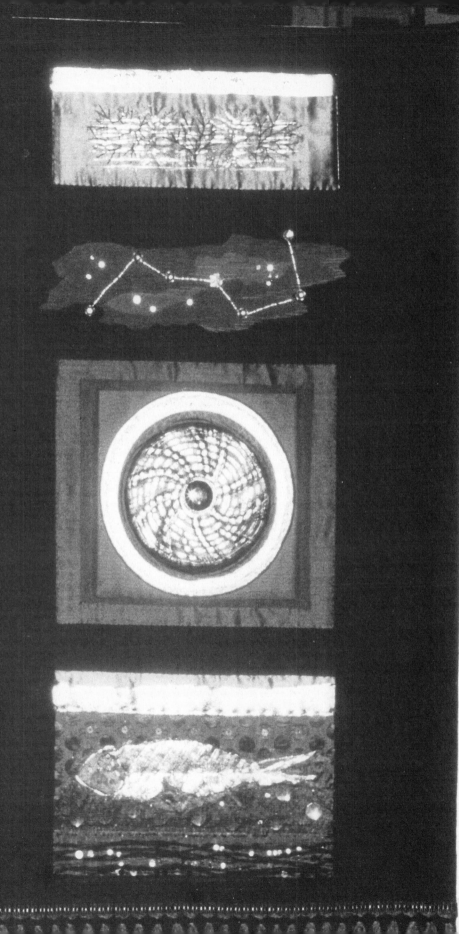

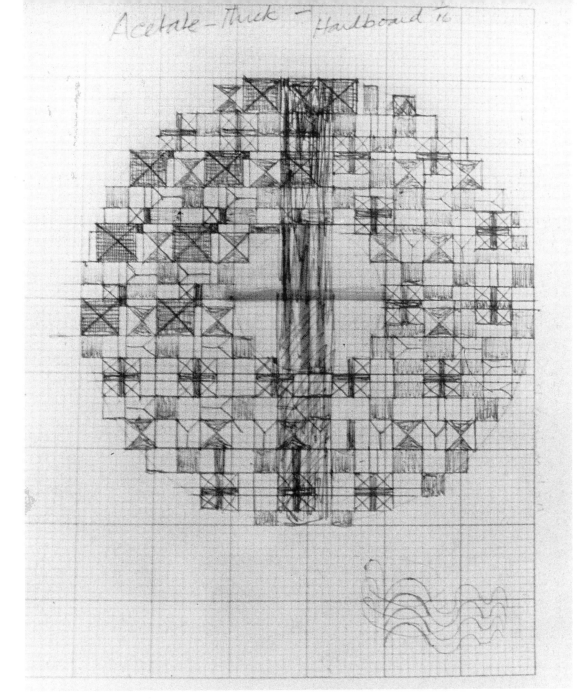

Acetate—Thick — Hardboard 16

88   Life Force, *lectern fall, 1960*
Deep green/black background with various
fabrics in dull gold, green, purple and grey,
with silver leather, metal thread and sequins.
No religious symbolism was to be used in this
commission so in the design were
incorporated symbols of plants, the firmament
with the plough, life force and at the foot a
fossilised fish, the hidden Christian symbol
Edinburgh Crematorium

89, 90 and 91   *The development of a pulpit*
fall, from the design drawn on squared paper
to the completed work. White silk
background with various fabrics in tones of
yellow and gold with gold and silver leather
and metal threads

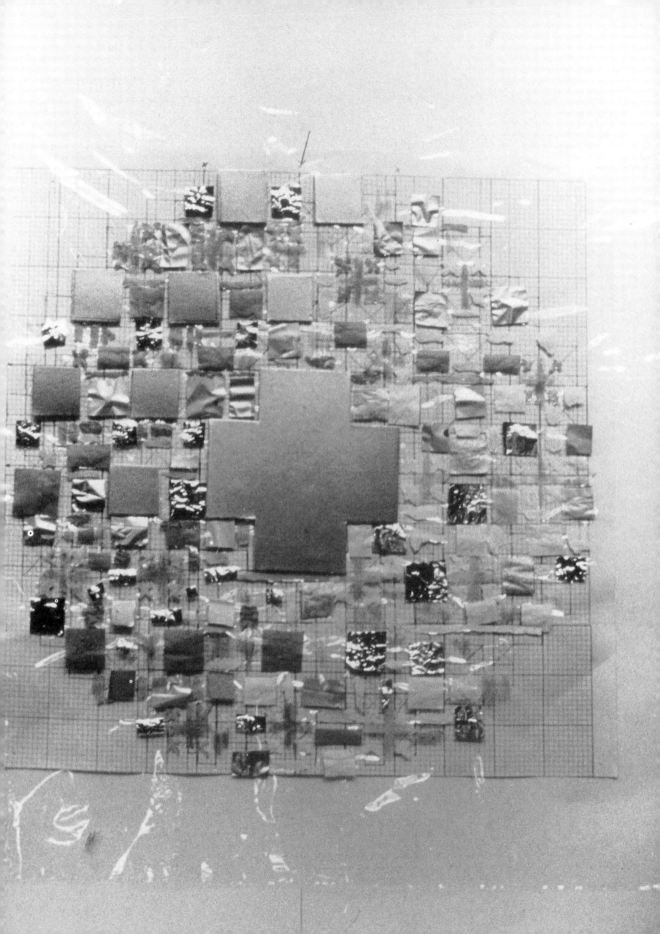

7 1974-87

92   Kathleen in the Department of
Embroidery and Weaving, Newbery Tower,
Glasgow School of Art, early 1970s

In 1969, while on holiday in Italy, Kathleen began to develop problems with her eyesight which was diagnosed as cataract. Before her eyesight deteriorated too far she took the opportunity to do intricate gold work and began *Abalone* early in 1975 (*94, 95, 96*). Initially it was a free hanging composed of quilted areas with details constructed of richly coloured layers of chiffon and gold threads. Although this piece was conceived in an attempt to break way from framed embroidery, she was never completely satisfied with it and later dismantled it to form five individual pieces entitled *Nacre* (Colour plates 7 and 8).

During 1975 she was invited to do a lecture tour of Canada visiting Brantford, Calgary and Vancouver, but on this tour her eyesight caused

93   Taormina *1969*
Cream flannel with silk threads mainly in surface darning.
Based on a crayon drawing done in Sicily.
5 × 8 (12.7 × 20.3)
Mrs Betty Semple

considerable difficulty. While waiting to undergo surgery she continued to work despite ever failing sight, adapting stitches and designs as necessary. *Whipping Tops* (*97*) is a large embroidery worked on canvas, the background of interwoven wools and cottons with the design created by 'ropes' of wool. The idea was suggested by the movement of spinning tops, both the revolving movement and the lateral movement, and the string used to whip the top. This

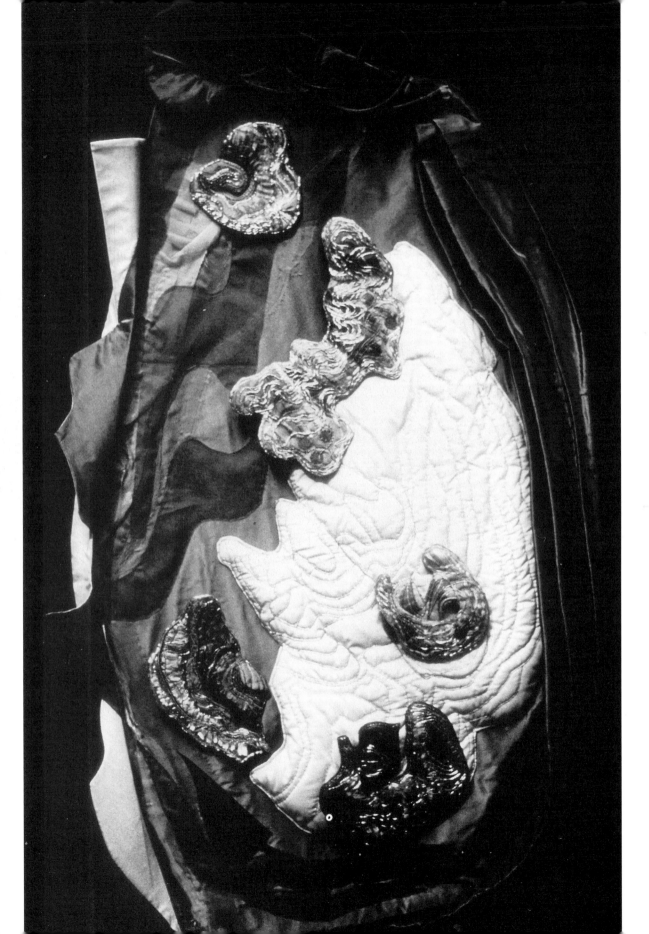

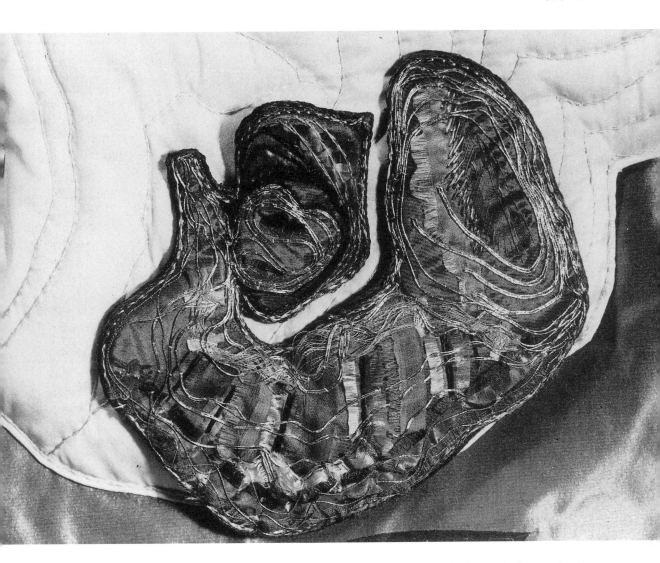

94   Abalone 1975 *(now dismantled)*
*Silks, cottons, shot taffetas and transparent
fabrics, with layers of fabric and richly
detailed quilting which give direction and
structure to the five smaller, intricately
worked areas.*
Approximately 48 × 30 (122 × 76)

95 and 96   *Details from Abalone which are
padded and built up in silks and chiffons on
subtle colours and tonal changes and with
metal threads. The five details were
remounted individually into satisfying
compositions, an exercise which Kathleen
found fascinating. See colour plates 7 and 8*

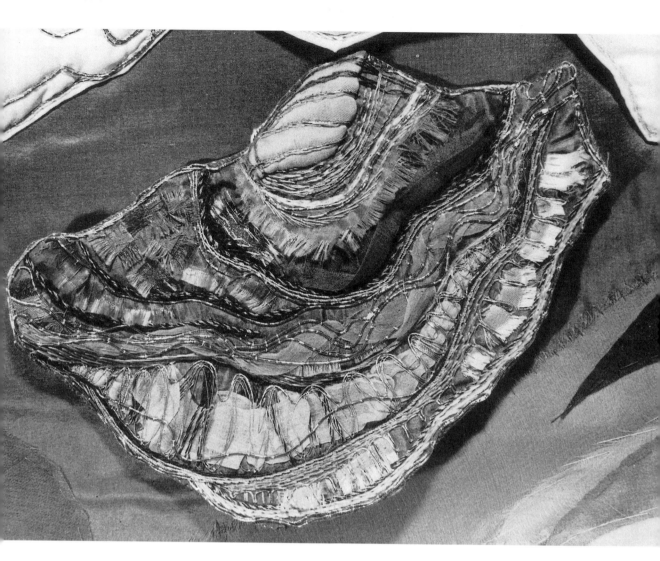

movement is interpreted through the vertical arrangement of the four diamond shaped tops and the rhythmical horizontal whiplash curves which link them as they whirl through thick bands of colour. The repetitive task of whipping the top to keep it spinning is suggested by the repetition in the design and the movement and underlying idea is further enhanced by the couching technique, used boldly for ease of working and also used because it gives the impression of blurred outlines and suggests that the ropes of wool are themselves whipped.

Again, as with so many examples of her work, this piece bears out Dorothy Angus's observation that she takes each idea further than one would expect, exploring and developing the subtleties, yet she is not afraid to state the obvious. Kathleen herself has often said that she is most interested in the completeness of the thought behind each embroidery.

Another piece of work from 1975 is *Honey Bees* (98) which resulted from an experimental stitch sampler on Binca (99). The adaptation of herringbone stitch was then worked in rows on heavy canvas with wools and loosely twisted silk

97 Whipping Tops 1975
*Canvas embroidered with wools and cottons
in shades of brown, yellow, orange, red, green
and purple. 54 × 18$\frac{1}{2}$ (137 × 47)*
Artist's collection

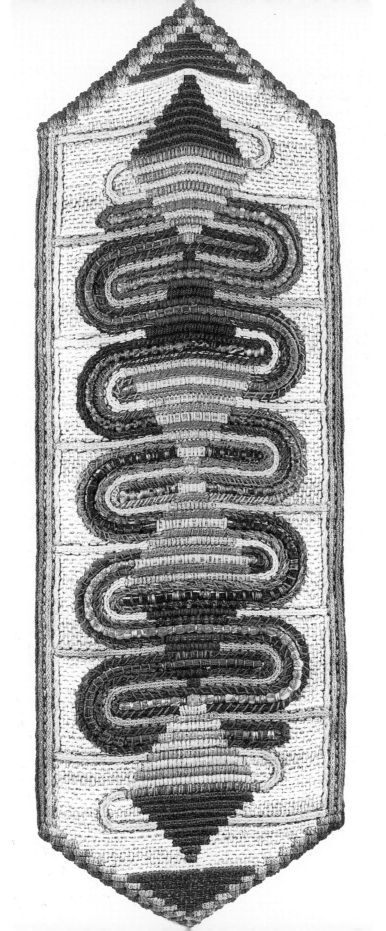

98 Honey Bees *1975*
Natural woollen background with gold,
yellow, orange and grey silk and cotton
threads with metal thread. 33 × 12 (84 × 30.5)
Royal Museums of Scotland

99 *Stitch sampler for* Honey Bees *1975*
Inventive new stitch forms from which the
complete panel grew. $8\frac{3}{4} × 10\frac{1}{2}$ (22 × 26.7)
Artist's collection

100   *Stitch sampler for* Honey Bees *1975*
Heavy canvas with bows of gold and grey
perlé cotton and natural linen threads, with
dull yellow, orange and gold wools and
unspun silk darned in behind in two different
ways. $8\frac{1}{2} \times 12\frac{1}{2}$ *(21.5 × 31.7)*
Artist's collection

darned in behind in two different ways, to achieve contrasting colour, scale and texture (*100*). This was the last piece of work completed before eye surgery at Easter 1976 when one eye was treated, the other being treated the following year.

Because lens implants were not commonly made in 1976 Kathleen now has to wear thick spectacles with corrective lenses which have dramatically altered her visual perception. Although devastated when the original diagnosis was made, she subsequently seized the opportunity to use the effects creatively. However, she found the initial experience quite disturbing, especially when her description was met with disbelief or nonchalance by the medical profession. In an attempt to encourage doctors to pre-empt a lot of anxiety by discussing the effects with their patients she submitted the following account of her experience to a medical journal. It gives invaluable insight into her positive attitude and her complete absorption with embroidery and design.

'Following my operation I was immediately impressed by the changes in my visual perception, both with my spectacles on and off. The distortion and magnification experienced with aphacic spectacles are well recognised, however it was the behaviour of colours as well as the range of perceptual phenomenon which I found particularly fascinating and which caught my imagination. As artist and designer I have attempted to portray my experience in pictorial fashion and have produced a number of such pieces in various media. As a designer I am continually aware of many odd formations and shapes whenever they appear. So in my first post operation state, as well as being dazzled by the brilliance of spring flowers, like a vulgar seed packet, I was fascinated to discern movements of small circles, spirals, parts of chains, etc, against a white table cloth. These were so exciting to me that I had to attempt to draw them immediately. I then became aware that all points of light, direct or reflected, large or small, intense or subdued, appeared to me, when looked at

without spectacles, to have oval shapes standing vertically and ranging from those derived from large orange street lamps to intensely brilliant highlights on a chrome kettle, for instance. All were full of movement, various systems of movement and utterly fascinating. Each oval was quite compact and edged with a rather spikey fringe, some appeared sliced off at the foot making a shallow thimble-like shape, but inside each oval the movement went on. These were of course very difficult to draw, to record an impression for others to see. The basic pattern could appear with the oval as an elongated cellular structure with a feeling of depth and movement against which excitement built up rapidly as all kinds of small units moved across it. Chains, single or entwined in complicated knots, ladderlike tracks and occasionally broad dark bands rather like offcuts of film, alone or angled in pairs. A few vertical lines and drifts like shredded silk wafted across. All this punctuated by many dazzlingly clear bulls eyes in varying sizes and arrangements of circles, each with a very definite centre, some really rather like holes in a button. One motif which appeared early in the performance was a large oval shape enclosing a sharply pointed, curving sided diamond with a cluster of small circles in the centre, very like a design for a piece of jewellery.

'How to depict this filigree of movement? To convey even a crude impression to others was now my problem. What technique could I use? Since I was looking at a particularly large orange street lamp I decided to use a copper crayon on a dark background to draw the basic shape of the oval and the irregular foundation pattern within it. This worked quite well and gave a slight illusion of depth. I then got a long strip of clear acetate and painted the chains and spots and other effects on it, in black, keeping the pleasingly random order in which they appeared. Since the transparent strip with its motifs was much longer than the basic oval it can be drawn over it creating a feeling of movement, albeit much slower and less complicated than the varying speeds, often rising to a turmoil, which I see.

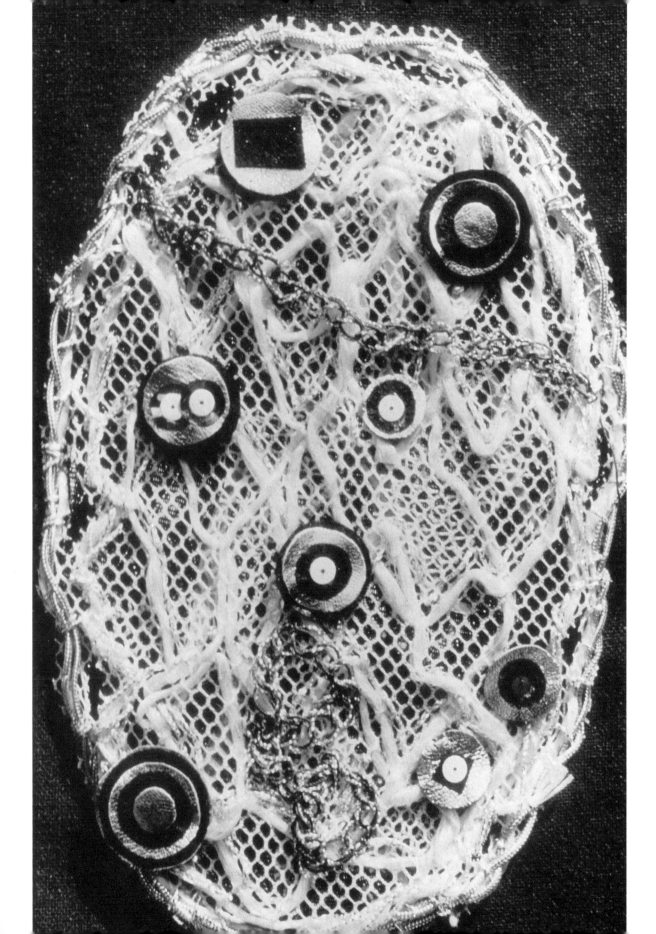

PLATE 1   Sea Maas 1931
Repp with wools, cotton and silk threads in a
variety of stitches which are built up to create
textural effects. 19 x 20½ (50 x 52)
Artist's collection

PLATE 3   Arbroath 1934
Tweed ground with three appliqué padded shell
shapes of corded silk, cream linen and white flannel,
the net all round the edge is of linen thread, the
details are in surface darning. 14¼ x 24¾ (36.2 x 63)
Exhibited at an Arts and Crafts Society Exhibition,
Burlington House, London
Artist's collection

PLATE 2   Icarus 1932
Detail. See illustrations 4 and 5

PLATE 5   *Sampler 1970s*
A variation of squared herringbone stitch worked
in wool, nylon, silk and cotton threads
5 x 5 (12.7 x 12.7)
Artist's collection

PLATE 4   *Weaving samples 1940-48*
Some woven at Ethel Mairet's Studio, Gospels,
Ditchling, and other are samples from garment
lengths woven in Aberdeen
Artist's collection

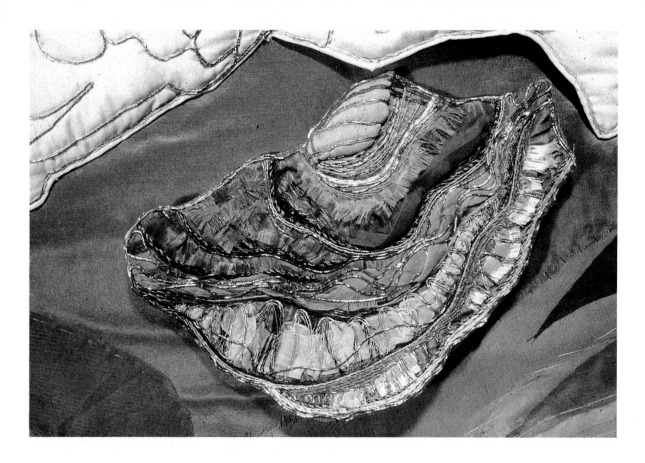

PLATE 6   Abalone *1975*
Detail. See illustration 94

PLATE 7   Nacre 1 *1975*

PLATE 8   Nacre 2 *1975*
Remounted details from Abalone.
See caption to illustrations 95 and 96

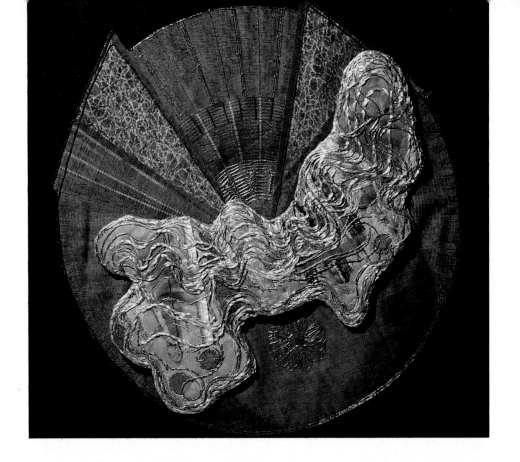

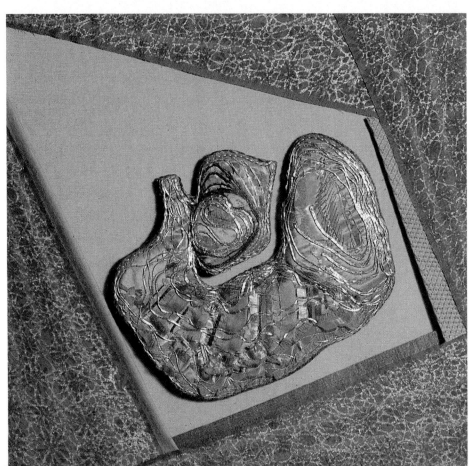

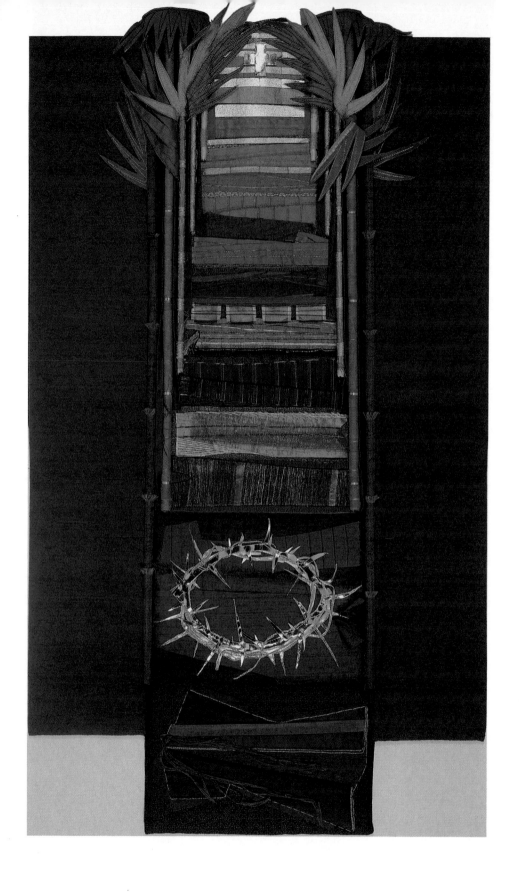

PLATE 10   Palm Sunday, *pulpit fall, 1979*
Detail

PLATE 9   Palm Sunday, *pulpit fall, 1979*
*Fragments of patterned and plain silks with machine
and hand embroidery and silver kid. The inspiration
for the design was the strewing of garments on Palm
Sunday. 34$^{1}/_{2}$ x 20 (87 x 51)*

PLATE 11 Poppies 1979
Scrim, silks and transparent fabrics on a raffia
background. 21¼ x 41¼ (54 x 105)
Mr and Mrs John Wallace

PLATE 12   By-Wash 1986
Various cottons, silks, rayons and felt with surface
stitchery. 26½ x 30 (67.2 x 76)
Artist's collection

PLATE 13   The Loch *1987*
Striped Indian silk, shot silk and chiffon with Italian
quilting in curving lines and stitchery with threads
drawn from the background. 19 x 15 (48 x 38)
Liz Arthur

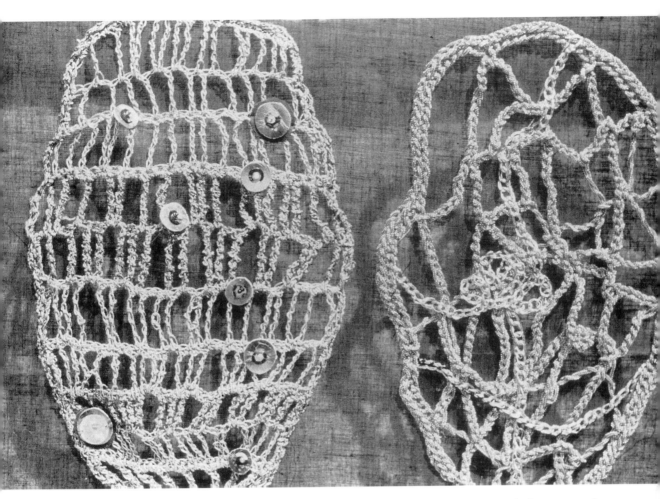

101 and 102   Samplers worked in an attempt to render visual disturbance and movement

'In this scientific age of wonderfully sophisticated equipment my rendering must seem more than primitive, but how other could I do it? I did make one oval in a large mesh white net and two others I crocheted, all quite successful in their own way and decorative to boot (*101, 102, 103* and *104*).

'My further observations concerning colours were noted on a brilliantly sunny day. A car headlamp catching the light acquired a new form, somewhat like a cornucopia or crocus shape and the thin tail being a strong blue purple while the rounded lip was yellow orange, leaving a large pure white area flanked by brilliant sparks. In fact all car lights at night appear somewhat like the above and this even when wearing spectacles.

'Another example of light being split up is rather difficult to describe. Again, it derives from highlights on a shiny surface. Imagine a bunch of fine rods bound together at one place and allowed to fan out above and below the tie, which in this instance is the point of light. The upper fan is filled with a complete spectrum, all the colours from purple at the centre spreading out to yellow at the widest spread of the fan, while the lower fan shape is quite different. All the colours have disappeared except bright red and bright green which alternate in thin lines with broad white spaces between. There were many versions of the fan shape all very much easier to render with white thread on a black ground than in words. This I found particularly interesting but hard to explain. . . .'

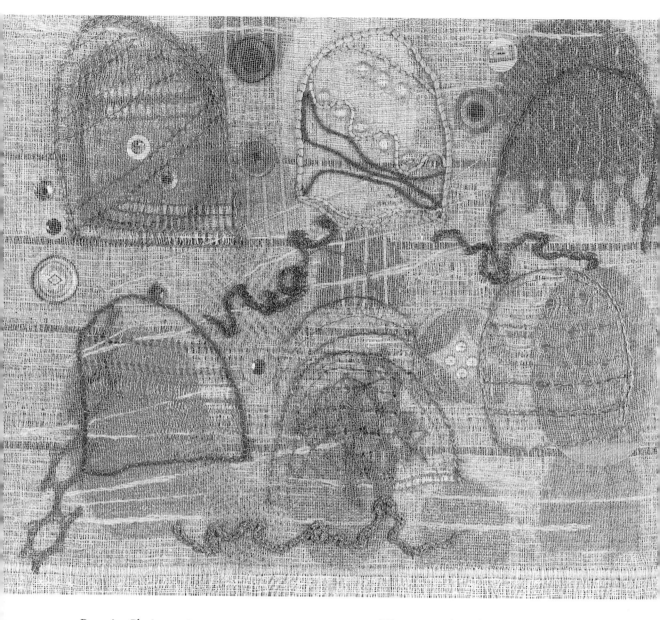

103   Protein Chains 1982
Two layers of fine linen scrim, white
underneath and natural above, prepared
separately in drawn and pulled fabric
techniques, gold fabrics, Shisha glass and
other effects trapped between the two layers.
16 × 20½ (40.5 × 52)
The Rev Iain J M Telfer

104   *Three samplers for* Protein Chains 1982
Two of natural scrim with gold thread, the
other of scrim with an orange weft and
turquoise warp on turquoise repp.
From a group of samplers each measuring
5 × 4 (12.7 × 10)
Artist's collection

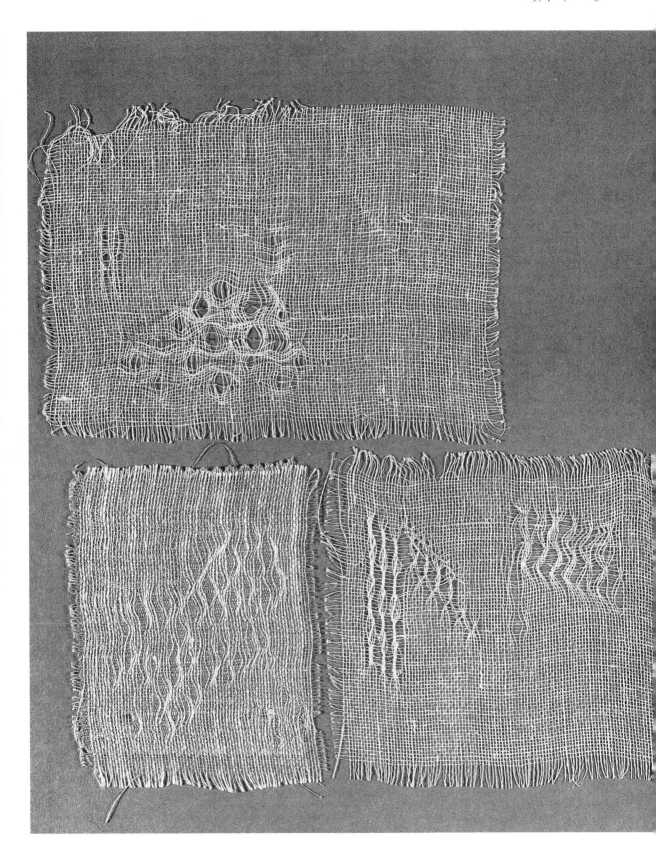

106   *Drawing for* Tree of Light *1977*

105   Stitch Tree *1977*
*White woollen ground with wools and silks in
shades of green, brown, orange, pink, grey,
turquoise and pale blue using straight and
rosette chain stitches.* $18\frac{1}{2} \times 16$ *(47 × 40.5)*
Artist's collection

The sudden perception of brilliant colours has
been caused by the removal of the cataract which
filtered out light, and the bright coloured spectrum is probably caused by chromatic aberration
of the spectacle lenses. Whatever the cause, she
remains aware of these visual disturbances and
more than ten years later continues to find them
fascinating, bearing out her own dictate that 'a
designer's vision consists of the ability in looking
at life to select and appreciate things for their
actual appearance quite unconnected with use
and association, to regard as beautiful the
strange contortions of a rusty old bicycle making
shadows in a puddle of dirty water or to find
stacks of trolleys in a supermarket a fascinating
essay in repetition'.[31]

She continued to explore the effect of light in a
study of a tree in her garden. After the initial
rapid crayon sketch she worked a panel using
wools and silks in straight and rosette chain
stitches on a white woollen tweed, retaining the

107   Tree of Light *1978*
Pieces of fine fabrics including printed silks,
nylon net, chiffon, silver net, silver leather and
shisha glass in shades of green, yellow, black
and white. The trunk is of layers of padded
and folded fabric. 28 × 33 (71 × 83.7)
Glasgow Museums and Art Galleries

108   Silver Thimble *1981*
Background of checked Thai silk in green,
pink and orange, silver leather and threads
with opalescent sequin waste. The outside of
the box is covered in green and purple shot
silk with silver yarn crocheted to imitate lace.
The outer edges of the motifs are covered
with grey chiffon to emphasize the three
dimensional effect. 17 × 13 (43 × 33.8)
Artist's collection

109   Sampler for Silver Thimble *1981*
Natural silk with a variety of sequin waste,
silver threads and leathers.
Each triangle is 1½ *(4) high.*
Total length 17½ *(44.5)*
Artist's collection

immediate spontaneous effect of the sketch
(*105*). She then went on to make a larger drawing
for which she made a small screen of net and
stippled through it (*106*). This was translated
into *Tree of Light* (*107*) using printed silks,
cottons, chiffons, silver net and kid with pieces of
shisha glass. This large panel was exhibited at
the second of the Embroidery Group's exhibitions to be held at Kelvingrove Art Gallery and
Museum, Glasgow in 1978, together with two of
the embroidered areas *Nacre 1* and *Nacre 2* from
the dismantled *Abalone*. (*colour plates 7 and 8*).

In 1981, to celebrate the Group's twenty fifth
anniversary, an exhibition entitled 'Argent' was
held in the Mackintosh Museum of Glasgow
School of Art. Kathleen Whyte exhibited *Silver
Thimble* (*108*), a fun, three dimensional embroidery nestling in a padded case lined with
Thai silk. The effect is of a precious, but larger
than life, object far removed from the mundane,
utilitarian item normally taken for granted: an
altogether appropriate symbol.

During the period 1978 to 1984 Kathleen
worked several small pictorial panels ranging
from *Dens Canis* (*110*) a delicate depiction of
dog's tooth violets, to pieces based on drawings
made during visits to Scandinavia and Orkney
(*112*).

One of her most recent embroideries is the
result of inspiration from nearer home. In 1986,
looking from her window across the village
green 'The Orry', she was struck by the dramatic